OXFO

TEACHING GUIDES

HOW TO

Assess Your Students

Making Assessment Work For You

ANDREW
CHANDLER-GREVATT

OXFORD

OXFORD
UNIVERSITY PRESS

Great Clarendon Street, Oxford, OX2 6DP, United Kingdom

Oxford University Press is a department of the University of Oxford.
It furthers the University's objective of excellence in research, scholarship, and
education by publishing worldwide. Oxford is a registered trade mark of Oxford
University Press in the UK and in certain other countries

British Library Cataloguing in Publication Data
Data available

978-0-19-841792-7

Kindle edition

978-0-19-841795-8

10 9 8 7 6 5 4 3 2 1

Paper used in the production of this book is a natural, recyclable product made
from wood grown in sustainable forests. The manufacturing process conforms to
the environmental regulations of the country of origin.

Printed in Great Britain by Bell and Bain Ltd., Glasgow

Links to third party websites are provided by Oxford in good faith and for
information only. Oxford disclaims any responsibility for the materials
contained in any third party website referenced in this work.

MIX
Paper from
responsible sources
FSC   FSC® C007785
www.fsc.org

Dedicated to John and Kathy, my parents.

About the author

Dr Andy Chandler-Grevatt has a doctorate in classroom assessment and a passion for assessment, teaching and learning. Having worked as a science teacher for ten years, of which five were spent as an Advanced Skills Teacher, Andy has a deep understanding of the pressures and joys of teaching in the classroom. Beyond the classroom, Andy has worked with primary and secondary teachers in a variety of contexts around the UK and in Canada, Kazakhstan and China. Alongside his national and international research in school assessment, Andy is a teaching fellow on the initial teacher education course at the University of Sussex, UK and is a successful published assessment author and editor.

Contents

Contents

Chapter 3: The future of assessment 207

Acknowledgements

This book represents the coming together of my attitudes, practices and beliefs about education over the past twenty years. Many people have shaped these, including my colleagues in the schools I have worked in, the learners who I have had the privilege to teach or work with, and the educators beyond the classroom. Without you, I would not be able to write a book like this.

The book exists due to the support and encouragement of colleagues at Oxford University Press: Amie Hewish for believing in me and involving me in the *Activate* project; Sarah Flynn for offering me the opportunity to write this book; Anthony Haynes for guiding me through the process of creating a book like this, understanding my temperament and keeping me focused; the three peer reviewers who gave me valuable feedback and encouragement; Karen Haynes for copy editing, which is no mean feat.

This book has been possible due to connections made through my talented colleagues in Initial Teacher Training, the Department of Education, University of Sussex, particularly with ex-trainee teachers who have provided me with case studies – Liz Cousins, Sue Pinnick, Jo Tregenza, Richard McFahn, and Rebecca Webb – and through the understanding and encouragement of my work wife, Fi Branagh.

Thanks so much for the significant engagement with the draft text and encouragement from: Katie Donaldson, Head of Science, Aldro Preparatory School for Boys, Godalming, Surrey, UK and Maxat Syzdykov, Nazarbayev Intellectual School, Kokshetau City, Kazakhstan.

The case studies have been provided by teachers who have been willing to share their experiences. Some have been anonymised or use a pseudonym. I wish to thank you all for helping this book come to life with real examples, with specific thanks to (in the UK): Corion (Coz) Crosby, science teacher, Ratton School, Eastbourne; William Beasley, teacher of English, Ellis Guilford School, Nottingham; Rachel Ind, Lead Practitioner Art and Design, The Warwick School, Redhill; Ana Cristina Merino Arnaiz, MFL (Spanish and French) teacher, Davison CE School for girls, Worthing; Heather Julia Wilkin, primary teacher, Cottesmore St. Mary, Hove; Thomas Murray, history teacher, The Angmering School, Angmering; Juliet Fulcher, primary teacher, Radnor House, Sevenoaks School.

Thank you to my Beijing team, particularly Lucia, Sharon, Song Ying 'Cassandra', and Leonard, and to my Kazakh colleagues, including, Zhangozy Ongarbay, Maxat Syzdykov, Narken Burkenov, Balaussa Yermenova and Viktor Sossin.

For help with the development of practice analysers, thank you to primary teachers Natalie Prince, Nicola Hunter, Charlotte Hastie, Katie Nolan, Emma Blythman, and Nusrat Nabi; to secondary teachers Micha Patman (drama), Catherine Bourn (science), Catherine Belbin (science) and Sheila Smitheman (maths); and to Georgia Newnham (early years).

Finally, Geoff – for being there, patience, belief and tea.

Chapter 1

Thinking about classroom assessment

1a) Personal introduction

I have been thinking about educational assessment for a long time now, probably for about twenty years. Longer than that – assessment was done to me as a school child and young adult, with some critical moments that I will share with you involving examinations, tests and assessments. As a teacher I started to question the nature of assessment in schools to the point that I began writing tasks that were alternative ways of assessing learners' knowledge, understanding and skills. I have come to understand that no amount of testing will enthuse or enable my learners to learn, and that learning actually happens between tests and examinations, within the four walls of a classroom.

I hope to convince you that my experience, projects and thinking give me something to contribute to your own understanding and practice of school assessment. Based on current educational research, its application in a range of schools and cultures, and my professional experience, I will demonstrate how you can change your own practice. There are many books that give tips for classroom assessment, with ideas for activities and strategies, but often without a real understanding of the political, social and cultural pressures at play in the school environment. This means that many of these activities don't appear to work for children or teachers, and often are not attempted again. If they are used, it is often in a tokenistic rather than embedded or meaningful way, in order to appear to be 'doing assessment' in the lesson. So, after outlining the principles of effective classroom assessment, the influences on the classroom, and a model with which to understand classroom assessment, I will present a number of strategies that can be implemented, and suggest how they will be most effective, given the cultural, political and social climate in which you teach. This means that your approach to assessment can change, enhance teaching and learning, and lead to better educational outcomes.

Finally, I consider the future of classroom assessment: how it may change and develop. I will present alternative approaches, as well as the challenges, drawing on a range of educational systems from around the world.

If I were to set myself some objectives for this book, they would be:

- Argue why meaningful classroom assessment is essential for effective learning.

- Recognise the influences that support and hinder good classroom assessment, particularly the cultural, social and political influences.

- Apply a model for classroom assessment to a range of practical strategies that can be used to improve classroom assessment, including planning, learning objectives and outcomes, success criteria, questioning, feedback, and student-led assessment.

- Emphasise how changes to teaching, learning and assessment can be changed in a range of educational climates, considering the cultural, social and political influences.

- Consider a range of alternative models for school assessment that could be developed and used in the future.

I am hoping that you, my readers, will be from around the world and will be able to manage changes to your own practice to improve teaching, learning and assessment in your classrooms.

I first realised that there was so much more to assessment than tests when I was in my second year of teaching. I was teaching science in a mixed-ability class of 11–12-year-olds. We had been learning about the particle model to explain the differences between solids, liquids and gases. On realising it was their day for homework, one of the keener students reminded me that it was 'homework night', and in haste, I came up with a quick suggestion to 'draw me a poster of an ice cube melting'. A week later, the class brought in their posters, which I settled down to mark.

The range of responses was incredible, from a drawing of an ice cube sat in a puddle of water, with 'ice' and 'water' labelled, to one with a melting ice cube with magnified area diagrams showing the arrangement of particles in a solid and a liquid. In between, there were posters that used keywords correctly or incorrectly, subtleties like including a thermometer to show temperature changes, and annotations that explained the details of particle behaviour.

I found that I could sort the posters into levels of understanding: those that had a basic, concrete understanding of the ideas, and those with a deeper, more conceptual understanding of the scientific process. There was a kind of continuum from basic to complex; some were clearly closer to the scientific model that I had intended.

At the time, late 1990s, we had an assessment system in England called national curriculum levels, which were descriptors of what students should achieve aged 13–14 at the end of their first three years of secondary school. I had been working with my mentor at the time on assessment using the levels; I had started to get a better understanding of the criteria. I was able to make a decision, in the form of a level, on each poster that was handed in. From this I could give feedback on what the students had done well, and the next steps to make improvements.

Fast-forward five years and I had changed schools and become an Advanced Skills Teacher (AST), specialising in formative assessment. At the time, our government had put in place an opportunity for excellent teachers to attain classroom-based promotion, rather than take the leadership route. I was assessed through portfolio, interview, lesson observation, and testimonials from my learners and some of their parents. ASTs were expected to teach at an 'excellent' standard and share good practice within and between schools. The media called us, rather sensationally, 'super teachers'! It was a great position: it provided lots of learning opportunities for me and my colleagues and had direct impact on my classroom practice too. The downside was being put on a pedestal and never feeling good enough.

By that time I had formalised the 'national curriculum levels' approach to assessment, by accompanying open-ended tasks with a simple rubric called a 'level ladder'. A level ladder listed the criteria to achieve each national curriculum level. The criteria were supposed to be as student-friendly as possible, so that learners could understand what they needed to know, understand and do for each level in a particular topic.

These level ladder tasks[1,2] were subsequently published in six resource books and used in many schools in England, as well as Wales, Ireland and British schools in Europe. Many science teachers used level ladders in their lessons in place of tests. During that time, what was to become one of the most influential education research papers was published. Paul Black and Dylan Wiliam, two well-respected researchers in education, conducted an in-depth review of current assessment practice in schools and identified the

[1] **A. Grevatt** (2005). *Badger Key Stage 3 Science Year 7 Levelled-Assessment Tasks.* Stevenage: Badger Publishing.

[2] **A. Grevatt** (2006). *Badger Key Stage 3 Science Year 7 Levelled-Assessment Investigations.* Stevenage: Badger Publishing.

advantages and potential impact of formative assessment.[3] In a teacher-friendly pamphlet, *Inside the Black Box*,[4] they summarised their findings, illustrating what they called 'a poverty in practice' in assessment. Many of the things that they identified I recognised in my own school and own practice. The crux of what they were saying was that teachers know what they teach (the inputs) and know how their learners will do in exams, but the assessment in the middle could be really improved. This idea became branded as 'assessment for learning' (AfL) in England, and has more recently been taken up in Kazakhstan and parts of China. The AfL movement changed thinking about assessment and, in many cases, changed classroom practice. Nationwide, teachers were aware of the term 'AfL' even if they were not doing it as well as it could be done. More of that later.

Now that level ladders were being used in science lessons across England and overseas, I was invited to give talks and training sessions at schools and local-authority events. It was great to meet so many teachers who were using these tasks, but I became increasingly aware that a significant number were not using the tasks in the way in which they were intended; they were being used as summative tests instead of an alternative, formative assessment activity.

Soon after this, I began a doctorate in education at the University of Sussex, researching how teachers used these formative assessment activities and exploring how teachers could be supported to use such activities more formatively. Doing a doctorate raised more questions than I ever expected, and throughout the five years it took me to complete it, I found that I questioned everything I did as a teacher. I came to realise how policy and politics influences education. Most importantly, I developed an understanding of social, classroom and school cultures and how teachers can influence them.

A couple of years after completing my doctorate, I was approached to do two projects that would challenge my thoughts about assessment and widen my worldview considerably. One was in Kazakhstan and the other in Canada.

Through a project with Cambridge International Examinations I was invited to participate in the development of the school-based assessment system with the new Nazarbayev Intellectual Schools (NIS) in Kazakhstan. At the time, I knew nothing about Kazakhstan, but since then have been fortunate enough to work with teachers in Astana, the capital, and a number of other cities in this vast and fascinating country. I proposed a criteria-based

---

[3] **P. Black & D. Wiliam** (1998a). Assessment and classroom learning. *Assessment in Education: Principles, Policy & Practice*, 5 (1), 7–74.

[4] **P. Black & D. Wiliam** (1998b). *Inside the Black Box: Raising Standards Through Classroom Assessment*. London: King's College London.

assessment model for use in classroom assessment, which was adapted and developed and is still being used. At the time, the education system was very focused on grades and examinations. What I learned from this experience is that there is no such thing as a 'blank slate'. Even if you have a brand-new system to implement, there are constraints on a number of levels – cultural, political and practical. I will share more of my experiences throughout this book to illustrate particular points.

In a following project, I was invited to be on an expert panel to design a school for 2030. This took place at a summit meeting called Learning 2030 at the Perimeter Institute in Waterloo, Canada.[5] The wonderful aspect of this project was the international panel of education experts, as well as learners from around the world, who were disaffected with their current education system. The networking opportunities were incredible, and I learned from people from almost every continent. I was pleased with the outcome, since we designed a 'school' system that had lots of assessment but not grades or examinations in school.

From this experience, I realised that the teacher–student relationship is similar and so important, wherever you are in the world (I can't imagine a teacher being replaced by a computer any time soon); also that student–student relationships are enormously powerful. And the complexity of education became even more evident: education is not a science with an objective 'right' way; it is instead a tangled web of values, cultural assumptions, political ideals, and personal experiences. Everyone involved was passionate about education, but we were all shaped by our experiences – positive and negative – of the current (and not-so-current) systems. So even though this was supposed to be 'blue-sky' thinking, there were practical constraints and passionate views to balance.

Based on these experiences, I am writing this book to provide both theoretical reflection and practical guidance to improve classroom assessment for anyone involved in school assessment systems. There is a vast amount of educational research that points to how to improve teaching and learning using formative assessment practices. However, teachers and learners are constrained by cultural practices and political ideals that have to be navigated. I have come to realise that teachers have significant power to shape the culture in their classrooms. Through this book, I hope to help teachers see the constraints they face, the opportunities they have to improve assessment practice, and the benefit this will have on teaching, learning and educational outcomes.

[5] **M. Brooks & B. Holmes** (2014). Equinox Blueprint: Learning 2030. <http://wgsi.org/learning2030blueprint> accessed 31 August 2017.

Setup of this book

This is primarily a practical guide to classroom assessment. As I have illustrated, education is not an exact science, and there are constraints on what teachers can achieve. So, I have a set of principles I wish to share through illustrations of practical experience and current research. While the book is, above all, practical, it has a firm evidence base. My main argument is that teachers can change their practice within their own classroom to use more formative assessment practices, whatever the culture of their school or country. I argue that classroom assessment is a social process, and that this is different from the statistical rigour of high-stakes assessments such as examinations. I draw on sociocultural and social cognitive theories to support practices in classroom assessment.

The book's main theme is that assessment has to be 'meaningful'; that is, both teachers and learners need to have a shared meaning of what it is to learn, what they are learning, what success looks like, and how to improve. I encourage teachers to move from teacher-led approaches to more learner-centred and learner-led assessment practices. Not only will assessment become more formative, but learners will become more self-confident, self-reflecting and, ultimately, self-regulating.

Each of the sections showing how you might develop your assessment practice has:

- an introduction to the assessment focus of the section, to introduce the key principles and make the argument for meaningful, social practices

- a description of how the assessment focus fits in my classroom assessment model and links to other sections

- a practice analyser to help you identify the practices you do and what you could develop

- a series of practices that can be tried to develop your formative assessment culture

- classroom case studies to exemplify how the practices can be used

- a research case study that focuses on a relevant piece of educational research

- reflection questions to help you think about the section and apply it to your own practice

- a summary of key points.

You might think of this book as a sandwich: the guidance on developing your assessment practice fills Chapter 2. Encasing it are Chapter 1, which explains classroom assessment in current contexts, and Chapter 3, which briefly discusses the future of assessment in schools.

 Reflection

Think about or discuss the following questions:

- What have been your experiences of assessment as a learner?
- What have been your experiences of assessment as a teacher?
- To what extent do you agree that school assessment is more than tests and exams?

1b) Approaches to assessment

Once, when working with teachers in Kazakhstan in a workshop on formative assessment, we looked at the effectiveness of grading each child in every lesson in 'the blue book'. This is a tradition from Soviet education experienced by parents, grandparents and teachers themselves; all see the process as an important part of the education system. While trying delicately to encourage the teachers to think about how this summative system could be used more formatively, one said (via my interpreter): 'Why change it now? It's worked for me, my parents and my grandparents!' Often, teachers will challenge change because many education systems seem to change for the sake of it. However, this teacher made me appreciate that certain practices are deeply embedded in culture and are seen as part of the education system, whether they are useful or not.

There are many things teachers and school systems do that are in place because they have always been done, unquestioned. Ironically, one of those things is questioning itself, as Black and Wiliam illustrated. It's a deeply-held cultural belief that teachers ask questions – but the usefulness and quality of that questioning can often be questionable. Another practice is marking learners' work with ticks on the page, often in a red pen. This method accumulates to many a teacher-lifetime without any sound teaching, learning or assessment rationale, beyond 'teacher has seen your work'.

These approaches have been called into question and are being improved in some cases, and made worse in others. More of this in Chapter 2 in the sections 'Questioning your questioning' (2d) and 'Giving meaningful and effective feedback' (2g).

Why do assessment?

At this point, I suppose we should take a moment to consider what the purpose of assessment might be, and explore its role in school education systems. There is a fair amount written on this, but for this book I would argue that its purpose in most school systems falls into three categories: for learners to obtain qualifications; for monitoring learners (and teachers) towards those qualifications; and for the accountability of teachers and schools to public authorities.

Qualifications are often seen as the gateway to success and determinants of what you do in your life and career. As a broad-stroke model, I see that schools exist to educate children, usually to an agreed curriculum of some form that (hopefully) prepares them for the outside world of adult life and work. The focus of school education, particularly in the later years, is for learners to get as many qualifications as they can at the best grades they can. Better grades are often equated with better jobs and more money. For this reason, teachers and parents strive to help learners get the best grades they can and to be as successful as they can be in school. In Chapter 3 I will question this model, but for now, it's a good approximation of most schools around the world.

Assessment also has the purpose of monitoring how learners are doing within their school career, and, in some systems, how well teachers are teaching. Learners' qualifications and grades can be used to monitor the success of an education system. Governments often like to demonstrate the strength of their education policies by showing the increase in learners achieving particular qualifications. For some time, a measure was in place in England: the number of GCSE (General Certificate of Secondary Education) subjects attained at A*–C grade. Teachers often expressed the view that if grades went up, the government would claim that their policies were working, but that if grades went down, teachers would be told they weren't working hard enough.

In an increasing number of education systems, teachers are being held accountable for their learners' grades – some having pay or professional progression linked to their learners' success.[6] Focus has shifted from learner responsibility to that of the school and the teachers.

---

[6] **OECD** (2015). PISA results in focus. <https://www.oecd.org/pisa/pisa-2015-results-in-focus.pdf> accessed 5 September 2017.

Schools often have regular assessments in the form of tests or formal assignments that are used as a basis of judgement. When I set a test, I would always look at the grades, but also, while marking, the marks that learners got for each part of the test. I was able to see questions they were getting wrong and make mental notes. This is a form of diagnosis. It also happens in any assessment activity where a teacher is comparing learners' knowledge, understanding and skills with what is expected.

Over a longer period, making assessment judgements can help form a picture of a pupil's progress. Teachers often use mark books to track progress. I taught during the transition from paper-based physical mark books to electronic, spreadsheet-based ones. In both cases, these could track pupil progress and be used to notice trends. Electronic mark books can be coded to automate this, identifying learners who are below or above expected rates of progress. The purpose of diagnosis and tracking is to help the third and the most important purpose of assessment: intervention. This is where the teacher uses their observations from tests or assignments to modify their teaching and approach to learning.

The purpose of assessment is highly contested,[7] but here I have shared my assumptions, based on my reading, thoughts and experiences. On the level of the local education authority and school, the purposes of assessment can be seen as qualifications, monitoring and accountability. However, the focus of this book is on assessment that takes place in the classroom, where the purpose of assessment, I argue, should be diagnosis, tracking and intervention.

How do schools approach assessment?

During the Learning 2030 project, I remember a situation where I was quite affronted by a description of our education system. Each day we had a morning session that explored the issue we would be tackling that day. A video depicted schools as factory farms, with batches of children doing assessments on a conveyor belt. This cold, factory-farming image of children really disturbed me and, to start with, I didn't feel that this was representative of my experience as a teacher. However, when I calmed down and took a moment to think, I began to see the big picture. We have very specific constraints on our systems. In most schools, children are taught in classes (batches) defined by their age, rather than their stage of learning. They are forced through the system and have to be ready to get specific qualifications at particular stages. In some systems, we filter the learners off

---

[7] **P.E. Newton** (2007). Clarifying the purposes of educational assessment. *Assessment in Education*, 14(2), 149–170.

into different groups depending on their academic performance at school. Often one test at a certain age will determine their future education. Some areas in England have a system where, at the age of 11, children take a test to determine if they go to a 'grammar school' or just a normal state school – a single examination that has impact on children's life chances.

Who is assessment for?

Having been fairly successful in our highly examination-focused education system, I have done many tests and exams. However, in hindsight, it was more often the case that these exams were done to me. If I think back to my high school terminal exams, I remember being given a syllabus and ticking off each section as I read it (I was very studious). Despite this dutiful reading, self-testing and ticking, I had no insight into what success looked like, except when that envelope arrived in the summer, with A, B and C grades for most subjects, and a D for geography. (I didn't have a copy of the geography syllabus!) And while I took some active part in the exam process, many of my friends really didn't have any involvement in the assessment process, beyond turning up to do the exam after minimal revision.

Traditionally, when it comes to assessment, the learner has assessment 'done to them'. They are taught something, they are expected to learn it, and then they are given a test to see how well they have learned it. It is a linear model, with the teacher in control of the knowledge and the assessment. Often the child does not have any information about what success in the assessment looks like, beyond answering as many questions as they can correctly.

An alternative model is that assessment is 'done with' the child. In this model, the learner becomes part of the process; by sharing success criteria, practising and taking part in each aspect of assessment, the learner can take control not only of what they learn, but how deeply they learn it.

Professor Wynne Harlen, an assessment expert in the UK, presented the 'done-to' and 'done-with' models in diagrams that I have adapted in figure 1b1 to illustrate the position of the child (and the teacher) in the assessment process. Diagram A refers to a system of assessment conducted by the teacher: the pupil (hopefully) learns material and then is tested on what has been taught. The diagram represents teacher input and assessment output with little consideration of what happens in the middle. Diagram B places the learner at the centre of an assessment process made up of four stages before the learner goes anywhere near an examination. Between the stages of learning goals, collection of evidence, judgement of that evidence, and the response to that evidence, there is a mediation process between the learner and the teacher, where the process of learning is emphasised.

A) Teacher-led assessment

Input
- Broad educational aims
- Teacher input
- Textbook input

Evidence
- Results from tests
- Outcomes of other judgements

Report
- Against criteria or norm-referenced
- Summative result to learner, teacher and parent

B) Learner-centred assessment

Specific goals

Next steps

Learner

Evidence

Judgement

Figure 1b1: Harlen's contrasting models of assessment: A. teacher-led; B. learner-centred, adapted from W. Harlen, 2007, by permission of Sage.[8]

The chances are that you will recognise features of both diagrams in your own classroom. This is the first important point that I make for this book: for improved learning outcomes and, ultimately, improved performance in examinations, the student has to be part of the assessment process in the classroom. There needs to be a culture of co-ownership of knowledge and assessment between learner and teacher. The second important point is that assessment can be improved through different relationships between teachers and learners. In fact, the

---

[8] **W. Harlen** (2007). *Assessment of Learning*. London: Sage, p.120 and p.122.

shared values need to be modified, to result in a cultural shift in the classroom, in schools, in the education system, and in society itself.

Of course, the transition from deeply-entrenched traditional approach to a learner-centred one is problematic. This is the case for both learners and teachers. I have experienced the challenges of encouraging learners to take a more active role in the assessment process, and I have seen teachers struggle with deeply-held beliefs about their role with regard to teaching and assessment.

In my own classroom, I found that children struggled to engage with success criteria when I shared them; they would resist peer or self-assessment activities or not recognise the value. Often with self-assessment activities, my learners would protest that 'marking is the teacher's job' – a belief that takes some time to challenge and shift.

 Reflection

Think about, or discuss, approaches to assessment:

- In your context, to what extent is assessment 'done to' or 'done with' the learner?

- Have you experienced any cultural clashes in the classroom or with colleagues where the roles of the teacher or learner have been challenged?

- What is the purpose of assessment in your school context?

1c) Summative and formative assessment

When I first gave thought to summative and formative assessment, it was in terms of a pretty clear-cut dichotomy. Summative assessment was to do with testing, scores and grades; it involved a 'sum' of some kind. It is assessment *of* learning. The opposite was formative assessment, where assessment becomes part of the learning process and has a feedback function – what has come to be known as assessment *for* learning. However, the more I have read, thought and practised assessment, the more complex the relationship between summative and formative assessment has become.

It helps, I think, to start with some of the main arguments developed in the most influential educational research paper for some time, the aforementioned work by Black and Wiliam[9] called 'Assessment and classroom learning', published in 1998. At 67 pages, it is lengthy for an academic article.

This paper was a review of all the existing peer-reviewed published literature on classroom formative assessment from around the world. Using the evidence from the 250 relevant studies found, the authors formed conclusions about classroom assessment practice and the value of classroom formative assessment on learning gains, with specific focus on good-quality feedback and pupil self-assessment.

Black and Wiliam identified four areas that they considered as problematic: current assessment did not encourage effective learning; summative assessment was having a negative impact on motivation; assessment had a managerial role rather than a role in learning; and finally, a focus on norm-referencing rather than criterion-referencing. I am going to expand on each of these and reflect on my own experiences to illustrate these points.

On the whole, classroom assessment was shown to 'encourage superficial and rote learning' where learners recalled 'isolated facts' which they soon forgot. This resonates with how I taught lessons in my early career. I was expected to give my classes a test on a topic every three to four weeks, so I soon realised that I needed to look at the test ahead to ensure that I had 'covered' everything. Now, even if I had 'covered' everything, by which I mean we had done a lesson on it, I was aware that the learners had not learned it. So I would find some quick fixes – to start with, in a revision lesson, but eventually throughout my teaching. For example, I used some well-known mnemonics, such as ROY-G-BIV or 'Richard of York gave battle in vain' for the colours of light in the spectrum (red, orange, yellow, green, blue, indigo and violet) and 'my very easy method just speeds up naming planets' for the order of the planets (Mercury, Venus, Earth, Mars, Jupiter, Saturn, Uranus, Neptune and Pluto). Yes, I'm old enough to remember when Pluto was classified as a planet.

Now, these were great for remembering facts in the short term, but by the time the learners got to their significant exams five years later, they had often remembered the mnemonic, but not what it stood for. This was particularly so if the knowledge had not been applied or revisited in those years. As I described earlier, from my personal experience as a student when I did my terminal exams, I learned by rote and forgot much of it soon after.

---

[9] **P. Black & D. Wiliam** Assessment and classroom learning. *Assessment in Education: Principles, Policy & Practice*, 5(1), 7–74.

Black and Wiliam's second claim was that questions used in teaching are rarely reviewed or reflected upon, and so lack focus in assessment. I will be discussing questioning in Chapter 2; however, for illustration, I will share with you an issue I commonly find when observing trainee teachers in the classroom. Early on, they will often fall into the trap of doing question-and-answer sessions with the whole class. They will stand at the front and ask a question; if they are lucky, a learner may raise their hand with an answer, without shouting out. The trainee teacher might get the correct answer and ask another. This part of the lesson often goes on for longer than the five minutes the teacher had allowed. Only a few learners are taking part, the others get restless, the teacher asks more and more closed questions, may veer off in a new direction to deal with a wrong answer – and the session ends up taking 20 minutes without any significant learning gains for many, or any, of the learners. On the trainee's lesson plan, the section is often labelled as 'question-and-answer session'; however, because the actual questions are not planned, they become unfocused and often have no clear purpose. It is not just verbal questioning that can lack focus. Questions selected from textbooks, worksheets and ready-made slides for projection also may not be focused on the learning objectives of the lesson.

The article's third claim was the overemphasis on grades and outcomes rather than the process of learning. If I think of the approaches I see in secondary science, often a topic takes six one-hour lessons, one of which will be the topic test and, maybe, one a revision lesson. So only two thirds of the topic time is devoted to teaching and learning, with one third for test preparation and the test itself. If, instead, there is a focus on learning that enables learners to make progress through reflection, feedback and improvement, there are far more learning opportunities, and that can lead to success in fewer summative tests.

The final claim was that a normative approach to assessment can lead to competition between learners, rather than personal improvement. This has a demotivating effect, particularly on learners who are less successful in the classroom. I will discuss this further in the final section of Chapter 2. The level ladder approach I developed used criteria-based assessment instead of a normative scoring system that is based on ranking students. Criteria-based assessment meant that learners had something concrete to aim for, with some specific guidance, rather than an abstract score or grade.

With regard to motivation, there has been a rise in the application of self theories, specifically the growth mindset. Black and Wiliam's claim that giving grades alone had a demotivating effect on learners has since been developed further using the theories of growth mindset by Stanford University Professor of Psychology, Carol Dweck[10] Growth mindset fosters a more 'can do' approach to learning, where success is achieved through hard work and intrinsic rewards (such as a sense of accomplishment). A fixed mindset, on the other hand, focuses on extrinsic rewards such as grades and peer recognition, and often has the default understanding that people have fixed intelligence and ability that cannot be altered, no matter how hard they work.

You might think that things may have changed in the two decades since 1998. Although there have been significant shifts in some places, it seems to me the overall picture has not changed that much. This is not the fault of teachers, more the policy landscape that surrounds teaching and schools. Many of the solutions that Black and Wiliam offer are as relevant today as back then. In their review paper, they took time to describe eight papers in detail that offered evidence of the effects of formative assessment. I want to highlight the key features that have relevance to the foundations of my thoughts. These papers all included quantitative studies that demonstrated learning gains. Three of the papers used mastery-style approaches, where the teacher believes that all learners can achieve, and uses test data to intervene until the learner can reach the pass mark. A particularly significant paper by Ruth Butler, a psychologist, showed that giving students feedback through written comments only was far more effective than giving grades or grades plus comments as feedback.[11] The other papers demonstrated the positive effects of goal setting, learner self-assessment, learner evaluation and opportunities to improve.

As a result of their review, Black and Wiliam presented the following findings:

- Current practice favours summative assessment.

- Formative assessment is poorly understood by teachers.

- Research has to be linked with a programme of intervention.

- To be successful, formative assessment relies on perceiving a gap between desired goal and present state and then the action taken to achieve the goal.

- Formative strategies do lead to improved performance.

- There is no single, definitive approach to formative assessment.

- Feedback is an essential component of formative assessment.

---

[10] **C.S. Dweck** (1999). *Self Theories: Their Role in Motivation, Personality, and Development*. Philadelphia: Psychology Press.

[11] **R. Butler** (1987). Enhancing and undermining intrinsic motivation: the effects of task-involving and ego-involving evaluation on interest and involvement. *British Journal of Educational Psychology*, 58, 1–14.

The key findings I will develop in Chapter 2 are that formative assessment relies on recognising the gap between the current state and desired goal and that this gap can be reduced with good-quality feedback and opportunities for students to improve.

Summative assessment bad, formative assessment good?

It certainly is not the case that summative assessment is bad and formative assessment is good, but, as Black and Wiliam argued, when summative assessment practices dominate in a system, they can cause missed opportunities for formative assessment and, at worst, have detrimental effects on motivation, learning and attainment. Summative assessment is not the villain, but in some situations it can have some unfortunate side effects. Summative assessment has its specific role in the education system: we need a moment to evaluate progress and assess attainment. Most education systems have terminal examinations that lead to qualifications. Accepting this status quo (I will offer alternative models in Chapter 3), summative examinations provide a benchmark through which judgements can be made for next steps in careers or job applications.

When I first talked to people about formative and summative assessment, someone remarked that 'weighing the cow doesn't make it fatter'. This is, of course, true – it's how you feed and care for the cow that will help it grow and put on weight. The same goes for our learners. Testing in itself does not make students learn; it might force them to revise and learn in the short term, but often the time is better spent 'feeding and nurturing' our students with good-quality teaching and learning.

If learners spent the majority of their school years just learning through formative approaches, they would build the knowledge, understanding and skills required, develop self-confidence, and self-motivation. However, most schools set regular tests to check and monitor progress. This means that learners are often taught to the test, spend a lot of time preparing for a test, and often will be just getting grades and comparisons with one another. So, in the classroom, I advocate teaching, learning and assessment that foster formative values.

As you might have realised, my original dichotomy between formative and summative assessment is not as clear cut as I first imagined. Is 'formative assessment' a label for a particular category of activity (a 'formative assessment task' versus a 'summative assessment task')? Formative assessment as noun – as fixed object? Or is it used as a verb, as a 'doing' word – 'we are doing a formative assessment activity', or even, 'we are using this activity for formative assessment'?

I have come to realise that classroom assessment is a way of working, a particular pedagogy. By this I mean it is a collection of values, attitudes and practices. Assessment activities can be used formatively or summatively – this depends on the values, attitudes and practices of the teacher and the learners. This I can illustrate from the research from my doctorate.[12] When asking teachers how they used the 'level ladder' assessment tasks, I was able to characterise three types of teacher: the teacher with summative values; the teacher with formative values; and the teacher with both values. Each was using a level ladder activity, but how they used it was very different.

The teacher with summative values

This teacher uses the assessment task in test conditions, where the learners are not able to talk to each other or draw on other resources. In setting the task in this way, the teacher considers the activity to be like a test or an exam, done independently by the learner. When the learners have completed the activity, the teacher collects the learners' responses and marks them, assigning a grade. This illustrates that the teacher is very much in control of the 'assessing' in the classroom. If you look at Harlen's two models in figure 1b1, it is clear that model A fits here: the assessment is being done *to* the learners.

The teacher with formative values

The formative teacher uses the task in a different way. They allow the learners to work collaboratively, where each produces their own response, but will talk to one another about the task, and draw on other resources such as their textbooks or exercise books (class books). The assumption here is that, in classroom assessment, learners can still actively learn. The learners can draw on other sources to fill in any gaps in knowledge, understanding or skills.

The teacher then ensures that the learners have an opportunity to peer assess or self-assess their work using the shared success criteria. This is giving learners a clear role in the assessment process. They are given the opportunity to use the assessment criteria to judge their own progress and identify areas for improvement.

Finally, after self- or peer assessment, learners have a chance to make improvements to their work. This is a moment where learning happens; the learners have moved on in their knowledge, understanding or skills.

---

[12] **A. Chandler-Grevatt** (2010). The use of levelled assessment tasks and their impact on teaching and learning in science education. Doctoral thesis (EdD), University of Sussex.

Although the learners are central to the assessment cycle and they are part of each step, the teacher's role remains crucial. They have planned the lesson to ensure that learners have the opportunity to engage with the success criteria, compare their work with the success criteria, and make improvements in the lesson. In addition, the teacher's values and attitudes are communicated with the learners. They have created an environment where learning is valued, improvement is encouraged and collaboration is promoted. This is much more in keeping with Harlen's model B (figure 1b1), and has several of the features listed in Black and Wiliam's key findings.

The teacher with both values

When using level ladder assessment tasks, few teachers exhibited purely summative or formative values, attitudes or practices. Instead, they used a combination of practices – sometimes with conflicting values. Teachers would often allow learners to do the task using their textbooks and class notes to look up things they did not remember. Occasionally, teachers would allow learners to peer assess or self-assess before handing in their work. The teacher would always check their assessment. These were conflicting values, since the teacher was giving the learners a bit of independence, but was ultimately in charge of the assessment process. Were they just giving learners some freedom, or implementing some formative practices, or maybe moving from holding purely summative practices to becoming more formative? Perhaps what I found was part of a journey of changing practice.

So, this section has described my journey from a simplistic understanding of summative and formative assessment to realising it is rather more complicated, and to accepting that both have a place in an education system. However, the focus of this book is that for classroom assessment, teaching and learning, it will be effective if teachers and learners tend towards holding more formative attitudes, values and practices. In Chapter 2 I will be considering how to foster these ideals.

1d) Teaching, learning and assessing

In a recent conversation with Simone, a trainee teacher I had just observed, I asked what she thought her class of 12–13-year-olds had learned in that lesson. Simone cited the objectives she had planned, so I asked her how she knew. Her reply was, 'because I told them'. It's a common frustration for teachers that just because we have told our classes something, it does not necessarily mean that they have learned it. Classroom assessment strategies can ensure that teaching turns into learning.

Part of my job involves teaching a few hundred trainee teachers in a lecture theatre. In these situations I feel like I am just 'telling', not teaching. Although I include a few activities to engage my audience, I really have no way of knowing if they are learning, or what they have learned by the end of the 50 minutes. Around the world, many school classrooms operate on a similar model, with the teacher at the front telling the learners what they need to know, and the learners dutifully writing it down. So, when does telling become teaching? A teacher is not that effective if they just tell their student what they need to know. A teacher makes judgements when the student responds to the teaching. The teacher checks if the student understands, may suggest ways in which to understand, and offers alternative approaches or ways of thinking. These, I argue, are the assessment aspect of teaching and learning. The teacher also makes judgements about what to teach next, the readiness of the student to 'take the next step', and any support they may need.

In the ideal situation, the student is motivated to learn, but in classroom situations it may be that the student is not engaged or motivated. The teacher recognises this and then uses motivational strategies to engage the student to want to learn. This, again, is a form of assessment – one that does not feature in an examination paper.

The student is not a passive receptacle. Assuming they have the motivation to learn, they too will make assessment judgements as to whether they understand what they are being taught, which parts they do and do not understand, and may come back with their own interpretation. They may not 'get it' and require help with how to learn about or do something. In the UK, there has been a movement that looks at how to teach learners to learn, which has been found to be effective when used in conjunction with formative assessment practices.

Teaching, learning and assessing as social activities

There is some interesting research into the nature of assessment in the classroom. Two studies in particular have had a huge impact on my thinking and approach to assessment. Both projects used sociocultural theory to understand the processes involved in classroom assessment. Sociocultural theory considers social processes and cultural values that influence, in this case, education. It focuses on the behaviour, practices and values in the learning environment. After describing each project, I'll draw on some findings from my research about classroom assessment.

The first project was carried out in the mid-1990s in English primary schools by Harry Torrance and John Pryor[13] (I still work with John at the University of Sussex, where he is now a professor in education). They were interested in the interactions between teachers and learners in the classroom, recording conversations during assessment events and then analysing them. From their research, Torrance and Pryor identified two versions of formative assessment. These two forms they called *convergent assessment*, which aims to discover whether a learner knows, understands or can do a predetermined thing, and *divergent assessment*, which aims to discover what the learner knows, understands or can do.

Torrance and Pryor argue that convergent assessment is not so much a type of formative assessment as repeated summative assessment. This manifests itself in the classroom in such practices as precise planning with tick lists and can-do statements, curriculum-driven judgements, closed or pseudo-open questioning or tasks (see Chapter 2, section d), and the pupil as the recipient of assessments.

Contrast this with divergent assessment, which involves the following practices:[14]

- flexible planning or complex planning that incorporates alternatives

- open forms of recording

- an analysis of the interaction of the learner and the curriculum from the point of view both of the learner and of the curriculum

- open questioning and tasks

- a focus on the miscues – aspects of learners' work that yield insights into their current understanding – and on prompting metacognition

- descriptive rather than purely judgemental evaluation

- involvement of the pupil as initiator of the assessments as well as the recipient.

In this case, assessment is accomplished jointly by the teacher and the learner.

---

[13] **H. Torrance & J. Pryor** (1998). *Investigating Formative Assessment*. Buckingham: Open University Press.
[14] p.152.

Although Torrance and Pryor do not suggest that teachers should adopt a solely divergent approach, they do assert that divergent assessment offers a greater scope for positive effects on learners' learning. These ideas are developed later by Black and Wiliam, who use the terms summative and formative, recognising that summative assessment dominates classrooms and that learning can be more successful if formative assessment dominates.

When I tried to apply these ideas to the level ladder activities, I found that the intended 'formative approach' was a combination of convergent and divergent assessment. On the one hand, the task is open-ended, but on the other, the criteria do give guidance of what to include in the assessment to be successful at different levels. The tasks do allow for different routes and flexible teaching, but the outcomes are established at the start of the activity. What is helpful is that the practices listed by Torrance and Pryor are very useful to keep in mind when planning for a classroom with shared formative values.

As my second example, Beverly Bell and Bronwen Cowie[15] have carried out a lot of research into teaching and learning in science classrooms in New Zealand. They too have developed sociocultural descriptions of classroom formative assessment processes. They make the distinction between teachers' *planned* formative assessment and *interactive* formative assessment. Bell and Cowie's model evolved through research that was first based on the *purpose* of assessment in science. Their descriptions and explanations of these processes are rich, so here I attempt to summarise their main points.

Bell and Cowie took into account features of classroom learning, or development, beyond subject learning. For them, the purpose of classroom learning is a balance of social development, personal development and science learning. In their construction of *planned* formative assessment, the *purpose* of the assessment is central to the relationship between the actions of the teacher and learner: the teacher *elicits* information using specific assessment tasks, *interprets* the information – often using science criterion-referencing – and *acts* on that information to enhance the learners' learning (figure 1d1). The teacher's actions could be focused three ways: science-referenced, student-referenced or care-referenced.

Their second form of formative assessment is interactive formative assessment, also illustrated in figure 1d1. Here the *purpose* of assessment is to mediate in learners' learning with respect to science, social and personal learning. This starts with the teacher *noticing* (described as faster

---

[15] **B. Bell & B. Cowie** (2001). The characteristics of formative assessment in science education. *Science Education*, 85 (5), 536–553.

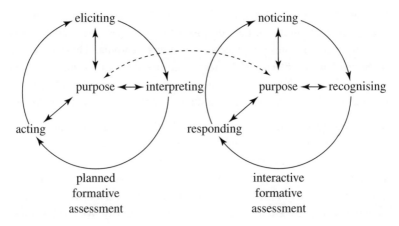

Figure 1d1: Bell and Cowie's model of formative assessment. Reproduced with permission of Springer.[16]

than *eliciting* in planned formative assessment), which collects ephemeral information (verbal, non-verbal and unrecorded). *Recognising* is the process by which teachers, through interacting with the learners, recognised the significance for the learners' personal, social or science understandings. Then comes *responding*: the process that happens in response to *noticing* and *recognising*. Bell and Cowie equate this to the *acting* aspect of planned formative assessment, but in this case the response is much more immediate.

No doubt you will recognise some or all of these practices in your own classroom experiences. Like Torrance and Pryor, Bell and Cowie have made reference to how formative assessment can be planned: this will be my first consideration in Chapter 2. For me, the most useful part of the Bell and Cowie model is indicated by the dotted line in the figure, showing that their two forms of assessment are linked. This means I can apply the ideas to lessons where planned formative assessment is present, but in addition, the interactive formative assessment takes place as part of the teacher's skill in teaching and assessing. The model highlights for me the importance of explicit planning for formative assessment values so that these can develop to become implicit parts of a teacher's repertoire of strategies.

Both these studies show the complexities of classroom assessment. Teaching, learning and assessing are interdependent processes: both teacher and learner have a role in each process. This was something I became interested in while doing the research for my doctorate. The experience taught me

---

[16] **B. Bell & B. Cowie** (2001). *Formative Assessment and Science Education.* Dordrecht: Kluwer. p. 91.

much about how an assessment activity fits into the teaching and learning, as well as within the curriculum and outcomes.

I started to think about the classroom climate for teaching, learning and assessment. This is really a way of describing the culture of the classroom from both teacher and learner perspectives. When considering the practices of teachers with different summative or formative values, I was especially aware that the classroom culture is created, not only by the actions that take place, but also by the words used. What the teacher says is as important as what they do.

This made me realise how the values of the teacher, and also the learner, had significant influence on how a task was used in the lesson. There were underlying assumptions about the purpose of the task and its role in assessment. These assumptions and values have huge influence on teaching, learning and assessing in the classroom. These influences I explore in the next section.

 Reflection

Think about or discuss the following questions:

- In your experience, when does 'telling' becoming 'teaching'?

- What, do you think, are your values and assumptions with regard to classroom teaching, learning and assessing?

- Having read about research studies on classroom assessment, what features resonate with your experiences?

1e) Influences on classroom assessment

So, if formative assessment is so effective, why isn't everyone doing it? I find this to be one of the most fascinating parts of being involved in education and researching how and why teachers teach in the way they do.

If we were to teach using the research evidence alone, we would not be communicating grades, but solely giving comments. Effective feedback would be central to our classroom routines. Teachers would be facilitating learning rather than transmitting the knowledge. We would have independent, confident, motivated learners, who would be successful in their school careers and beyond.

In England, in the early-to-mid-2000s, the government put a lot of investment into training teachers (both pre-service and in-service) in AfL. At the same time, a team of researchers and teachers were implementing the principles of AfL, which continued to demonstrate that changes in assessment practice could lead to improved learning for learners.[17] The teachers in these studies were supported by the research team and had bespoke training in instigating change (with permission from their leadership teams to do this). Schools, teachers, learners and parents were generally 'on board' and moving forward. Elsewhere, however, the embedding of formative assessment practices in classrooms across the UK was much more tokenistic, despite pockets of excellence.

The term 'assessment for learning' became one that was seen as important to be doing. Two researchers in England, Bethan Marshall and Mary Jane Drummond, characterised this as doing it 'to the letter', rather than taking on the spirit of AfL[18] This is when teachers do what is expected, not really understanding the underlying principles, compared with teachers who fully embrace formative values, assumptions and practices. School leadership teams can treat many education initiatives as the next thing to be seen doing, and the initiative becomes reduced to an instrumental change imposed on staff and learners. The benefits of a deeper, more embedded, commitment to the initiative are thus lost.

In this section, I want to show that teaching, learning and assessment have many influences upon them. The complex interactions of these will have an effect on what is assessed, how it is assessed, and the perceived value of that assessment. It's difficult to disentangle each of these exactly, but I have divided them into four areas of influence: research; culture; political; and social.

Research influences

When I started my doctorate, educational research seemed remote from classroom practice. Not until I had access to a university library did I even view educational research journals. And then many of the articles were thick with academic jargon. The ones I did manage to read often felt far removed from my own practice. However, the more I studied, read and applied the ideas I read about, the more I understood how educational research could

[17] **P. Black, C. Harrison, C. Lee, B. Marshall & D. Wiliam** (2003). *Assessment for Learning: Putting it into practice*. Maidenhead: Open University Press.

[18] **B. Marshall & J. Drummond** (2006). How teachers engage with assessment for learning: Lessons from the classroom. *Research Papers in Education*, 21(2), 133–149.

be used as an evidence base. Most importantly, I learned that educational research can inform educational practice.

It still amazes me that, some fifteen years on, teachers and schools in the UK are only just becoming aware of AfL and implementing ideas that were first shown to be effective over a decade ago. The educational research of Black and Wiliam is unusual in its impact and implementation. However, despite the efforts of the authors to influence policy, schools and teachers through an intervention programme, they did not succeed in completely changing practices and cultures across a national school system. Nevertheless, the AfL phenomenon has had far-reaching impact across the globe, and has arguably had greater impact on school-based assessment than any other educational research.

Educational research has a troublesome reputation, as it does not sit firmly as a traditional discipline – instead, it draws on other disciplines to make sense of the processes of teaching, learning and assessment. For example, I have drawn on psychological, philosophical, political and sociological theories to come to understand assessment in the context of classrooms, schools and educational systems. These ideas are forever evolving.

Having been a biologist, I spent the early part of my career thinking in the domain of natural science. When I was changing light levels and carbon dioxide levels on genetically modified tobacco plants for my master's degree, I had a clear hypothesis, used quantitative methods (mostly) and could see a direct relationship between the effects of these conditions on the plants doing photosynthesis and the expected changes due to climate change. During my doctorate in education, I had to move from a natural scientist's approach to understanding the world to a social scientist's. This was not easy, but as I have become aware of different ways of knowing, I have come to appreciate the complex world of education.

Through doing educational research, I came to realise why research evidence was poorly implemented into school systems. Not only do teachers not have access to the research, or the skills to understand and use it, but there are far bigger influences, assumptions and processes at play. This complex web is entwined through cultural assumptions and political ideologies.

For example, in a later paper, where they looked at assessment practices in other countries, Black and Wiliam were able to identify some of the complexities that affect how assessment practices are taken up by different countries, schools and teachers. These included:

- beliefs about what constitutes learning

- beliefs in the reliability and validity of the results of various tools

- trust in the objectivity of formal testing

- a preference for, and trust in, numerical data, with bias towards a single number

- trust in the judgements and integrity of one's children's teachers

- trust in the judgements and integrity of the teaching profession as a whole

- belief in the value of competition between students

- belief in the value of competition between schools – the market model of education

- belief that test results are a meaningful indicator of school effectiveness

- fear of national economic decline and belief that education is crucial to improvement

- belief that the key to schools' effectiveness is strong, top-down management.[19]

Beliefs, trust, preferences and fears: all these require social-science methods to identify, describe and explain. These emotions and attitudes come from cultural heritage, political backdrops and social experiences.

Cultural influences

I have been fortunate enough to visit several schools in Kazakhstan. When I first arrived in the capital city Astana, I found it the most alien place I have ever visited. I had taken time to read the few books in English about the country and to learn a small amount of Russian – I am at toddler level, I can point and name things – and even less Kazakh language. I have visited many Western cities, but Astana for me was different: the smells, the sights, the architecture, the roads, the airport, the appearance of the people. I loved it. It was completely outside my comfort zone, but it was amazing.

I remember being shown around a secondary school in which I was going to be training some teachers in formative assessment. It *felt* like a school; the corridors, the assembly hall, the learners bustling around their wall of lockers at break time. Once talking to teachers and students, often through an interpreter, it became clear that although I was in a completely different place, the teacher–learner relationship was still the essence of teaching, learning and assessment. The nuances were different, but the role of the teacher and the role of the learner were clearly defined.

---

[19] **P. Black & D. Wiliam** (2003). In praise of educational research: formative assessment. *British Educational Research Journal* 29(5), 623–637.

School culture in Kazakhstan is very influenced by Soviet and Asian cultures, though they have reached out and have attempted to take on some Western strategies.

Something that I noticed when working in Kazakhstan and China is the emphasis on certification. There are whole sets of bureaucracy based upon the production, signing and presenting of certificates. It's almost as if, without the certificate, you haven't done it. I even got a certificate for running workshops in Beijing; it's a very glossy, gold-embossed certificate in its own red case.

This emphasis on certification is part of the legacy of the *keju* system. More than two thousand years ago, the Chinese invented the examination. It became the *keju* – examinations in Confucian texts – which lasted for thirteen hundred years, until abolished in 1905.

Confucius was a philosopher, politician and teacher that I was soon to find is central to Chinese cultural, political and social life. When working with Chinese teachers in Beijing, I was told that language lessons in Chinese teach Confucian foundations of respect, humanity and rituals.

The Chinese official class was made up of scholar-officials. The *keju* represented the only way to become a scholar-official and work for the government – a highly esteemed job (and the only way to achieve social mobility in the dictatorial society). These examinations had several levels to progress through, for which successful candidates were given titles and privileges. Once retired, these men (only men were allowed to sit these exams) became moral examples, teachers and unofficial judges; their wisdom and learnedness were valued by society.

The *keju* system has been revered across most of Asia – many educational systems being based on this approach. Compare this with Western values of education, which go back to the ancient Greeks, such as Socrates and Plato.

Political influences

The big political structures, such as autocratic, democratic and semi-democratic, determine how much control is given to schools, education and assessment. I work in a democratic society in Britain. This has influences on cultural and social assumptions and on education itself. Education is seen by elected governments as something that they can change for the better, and is an easy target for ambitious politicians to provide a platform in their careers.

A country's political lean will have influence on the curriculum, school measures and assessment. For example, the more conservative favour more traditional curricula of established subjects, and the liberal more integrated ones.

Most governments pay great attention to their country's global position in education, using international comparison tables as the basis for making political decisions about education. We are in a process of globalising education by comparing education systems across the world. When I was in Kazakhstan, education officials, teachers, and sometimes even children would talk of 'world-leading education'. It is their aim to become world leaders and have a high-performing education system. Interestingly, those in China, which is considered world-leading in education, are more critical of their position, and there is a hunger to change traditional teaching to more creative, flexible teaching and learning. The UK is perceived as having a very good education system, regardless of its just-above-average position in the world rankings.

Unfortunately, in my view, international comparison tests are fuelling global competition – most significantly, PISA (Programme for International Student Assessment). PISA designs international tests that are taken by 15-year-olds from participating countries, and then uses these to rank countries in the performance in literacy, mathematics and science. Despite having some laudable features, PISA has created a culture where governments around the world want to prove that they are world-leading in education, and it is used as the benchmark to prove their success. This means that governments are keen for national curricula to meet the demands of these international tests and climb the ladder of perceived educational success.

Politicians or education officials often have a very large part to play in educational policy, but their decisions are rarely evidence-based and are more likely to be ideologically influenced. In most countries, decisions on education are made by people furthest away from the chalkface, (or often, these days, the pixel-face). Some countries, such as Finland and some states in Canada, have excellent policy makers who engage with academics, school leaders and practitioners to inform policy developments. Often, however, politicians will only call upon those with the same political agenda.

Teachers rarely have carte blanche to teach what they like. If I could teach what I wanted, I suspect my learners would always be doing some sort of plant biology, which is my passion. Not just experiments or microscope work, but also botanical drawing, the history of the great plant hunters, and so on. I'm sure that you have your particular passions as well. Perhaps luckily for my learners at school, I am constrained by a national curriculum. This sets out what I should be teaching learners at each stage of their schooling.

The curriculum will be the greatest influence on what teachers teach, what learners have to learn, and how these things are assessed. Many countries or states within countries have a curriculum imposed by the government. Usually, this is a document that states *what* has to be taught; fewer curricula state *how* the content should be taught, as this is usually left to the teachers.

So what teachers teach is constrained by what they are employed to teach, usually decided by a state body and likely to be influenced by the international climate of what is deemed as important 'knowledge, understanding and skills'. However, there is usually another dimension that is sometimes explicit and sometimes implied by a national curriculum. That is a set of values: cultural values (what knowledge and skills are considered important) and educational values – the purpose accorded to education, the way we teach and the emphasis on what is taught. This is often most explicit in history curricula, where history – even 'world history' – is taught from the national perspective. In science, in my experience, the same Western scientists are often used as examples, even in Kazakhstan. What does differ, depending on the priorities of the country, is a focus on particular health issues or diseases.

We have these global influences and the influences of the cultural values of a state; what we teach and what children learn is influenced by the way we evaluate such things and how we assess them. Globally, testing is the dominant mode of assessment. National tests and qualification examinations are the norm. Test results are under the scrutiny of governments, and many countries use them to compare schools and decide on whether teachers get a pay rise. All these uses and applications will affect how teachers use assessment in their lessons.

Social influences

Classroom assessment ensures that learners make progress through developing knowledge, understanding and skills. It is complex, multifaceted, and requires strong professional knowledge. Above all, it is a social process. By this I mean it relies upon human interactions through which the teacher and learner negotiate learning. Effective teachers have good professional knowledge to judge how well a student is doing, and intervene to help them learn and improve.

An effective teacher makes decisions not only based on their own knowledge of the subject, but also their knowledge of learners' learning in general, and knowledge of each individual student they teach. For example, a teacher of physics will be aware of the misconceptions that are common when learning about gravity, and so can plan to challenge them, or identify them when they occur. In addition, the teacher will know that Joe needs encouragement when tackling mathematical problems, and that Theresa responds well to being challenged by being given difficult problems to solve. The teacher makes decisions on how to teach, assess, and give feedback to the individual learners.

Teachers also employ discretion when marking work and motivating their learners to improve. Two learners may get exactly the same mark in a topic test, but the teacher may express disappointment to one who they feel has underperformed through lack of preparation, while giving praise and encouragement to the other, who worked hard, revised thoroughly and achieved beyond expectation. These are both social interactions, and are both related to motivating learners to improve.

 Reflection

Think about or discuss the following questions:

- How much access do you have to educational research? How accessible is it to you? What influence does it have on you?

- What political situation do you work in? What influence does that have on you?

- What are the cultural norms that you work with? What influence do they have on your classroom?

1f) A model for assessment

Through my various experiences, I have developed a working model that helps me make sense of the various constraints and activities involved with assessment in schools. Figure 1f1 represents this model, and will form the basis of the structure of this book. It draws on ideas I have put together from research and personal experience, and is much influenced by many great thinkers in educational assessment.

Let me take you through the outline structure before going more deeply into the details of the activities at each stage.

First, I want to draw your attention to the left-hand column, 'curriculum statements'. This is our first constraint, if you like. This is the specified knowledge, understanding and skills to be taught. Normally representing a national curriculum, this column could also contain an examination board specification, or curricula from an independent (private) school or other educational institution. In some cases, this may be content-focused;

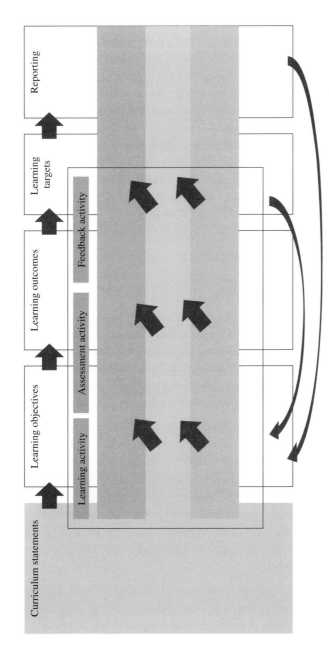

Figure 1f1: A model for classroom assessment

in others, skills-focused. Whatever it is, it forms the practical boundaries within which assessment will take place.

Next, notice that this column has a horizontal bar coming out from it, to form a sideways T shape. This bar can often be used as the benchmark of *how well* that knowledge, understanding and skills should be achieved by the end of a specific period. Notice that it is overlaying all the other columns. This benchmark is often informed by the national curriculum if it has some assessment criteria, though some lay it out as the blocks of knowledge to be mastered within the time period. For example, the 2014 national curriculum for England removed all assessment guidance and states that learners must have a 'secure' knowledge and understanding of the national curriculum statements. Previous to that, since 1998, the national curriculum for England had assessment criteria (called national curriculum level descriptors) for all school phases, which could be used in assessment.

The horizontal bars above and below the central 'benchmark' bar represent the knowledge, understanding and skills that are lower than the benchmark, or, conversely, go beyond it.

Now look at the vertical columns labelled 'learning objectives', 'learning outcomes', 'learning targets', and 'reporting'. The arrows between them show how each one informs the next. So, a national curriculum statement informs the learning objectives; the outcomes are dependent on the national curriculum guidance (or other sources); once assessed, the learning outcomes inform the next steps (targets) for the learners in achieving the benchmark; and finally, this information will inform a summative outcome for 'reporting'.

Reporting is a summative moment where some sort of data is recorded on the student's performance at a given time. Reports are often decided by schools, and are traditionally termly, when data is collected by teachers and often shared with parents. As well as monitoring student progress, performance data also can be used by school management for monitoring teacher performance. At state level, some governments require specific data following particular periods of schooling – often at the end of schooling (terminal exams), but frequently at significant waypoints, such as the end of primary education.

Notice the arrows that feed back at the bottom of these pillars. These represent that learning targets and outcomes of summative reporting should inform the next stages in teaching – that is, the learning objectives.

Now to the box straddling the columns that shows three processes. Between 'national curriculum' and 'learning objectives' is 'learning activities'; between the 'learning objectives' and 'learning outcomes' comes 'assessment activities'; and between 'learning outcomes' and 'learning targets' is 'feedback activities'. Note that these are enclosed in a box that is superimposed on the three horizontal bars.

This overlaid box defines a learning episode – be it a lesson, a series of lessons, or a topic. It is a period of time in which the learning objectives can be met. Traditionally, this will be a lesson, often one hour, where learning, assessment and feedback activities can occur. However, some topics, subjects or school systems may have a longer period in which this cycle occurs.

You may have already wondered where the word 'teaching' or 'teacher' is in this model. The teacher is intrinsically involved in the whole process; they are the architect of the learning, assessment and feedback activities. I could use the term 'teaching activities' instead of 'learning activities', but for me, the latter ensures that learning is the focus, rather than the teaching. What is the point of assessing something if a pupil has only been taught it, not actually learned it?

The 'activity' box in the figure is very important because this is where learning takes place – where the teacher can teach, assess and give feedback using a range of selected strategies. This is classroom assessment: the space where learners and the teacher are working together, creating meanings and co-constructing knowledge.

Reflection

Use the model of school assessment in figure 1f1 to identify the features of assessment in your context:

- What are the inputs and guidance given on what should be taught?

- What information do you have for assessment criteria? What would be your 'baseline'?

- What and when do you have to report?

- Do you have learning objectives, learning outcomes and learning targets? How are they devised? How are they used?

- Do you have learning activities, assessment activities and feedback activities in lessons (learning episodes)?

- Is there anything missing from this assessment model that exists in your context? Is there anything missing in your school assessment system that could be added?

Chapter 2

How to do classroom assessment

2a) It's not what you do, it's the way that you do it

I suspect, if you are a teacher, that you will have flicked through Chapter 1 and turned to these pages for the instructions of how to do classroom assessment. I know, I've been there. We have limited time and we haven't got time to read the preamble; we need to get to the job in hand of actually teaching.

When I first produced the books of level ladders for science teachers, I wrote an introduction section of about twenty pages, detailing the best approaches, providing exemplars, and giving references. Not long after they were published, I was asked to go into schools to train teachers in how to use the tasks effectively. It turned out that I usually spent an hour presenting the introduction to the book – and teachers left feeling better informed and ready to use the tasks (in a more formative way). They just hadn't had time, or taken the time, to read the introduction. This is not a criticism of all the hardworking teachers out there; it is a fact of being a busy professional.

However, one of the reasons that classroom assessment can appear to be ineffective is because teachers do not fully understand it and have not had the inclination, time or opportunity to engage with the underlying principles. Some teachers are critics of worksheets or textbooks, and the quality of these is indeed variable (although, I would argue, the resource or strategy is only as good at the teacher using it). The reason that teachers are so important is that they know their subject and they know their learners; using both those knowledge bases, they can select and use resources in ways appropriate for their learners. This may mean presenting the resource differently, targeting groups of learners with different parts of the activity, or just drawing on the resource in a more appropriate way. If I had to summarise my doctoral thesis, I think I could say that, for Levelled Assessment Tasks, 'it's not what you do, it's the way that you do it.'

So, I would urge you to spend some time reading Chapter 1 if you can make the time, as you will then get far more out of the rest of the book. If that isn't a possibility, here is a summary of the main points I made, in the hope that you will get the gist of what I am arguing for:

- Classroom assessment is not about tests and exams. It is the process of teaching, learning and assessment between the teacher and the learners, usually within the classroom.

- Classroom assessment should be student-focused, with the learner involved with each process of the assessment cycle: establishing objectives and outcomes; review; feedback; and responding to feedback.

- Classroom assessment focuses on formative assessment strategies that can be teacher-led or learner-led.

- Teaching, learning and assessing are inextricably linked, and are part of a social process in the classroom.

- There are several influences on classroom assessment; for example, social, political and cultural. Although all can be challenged, some take more time than others.

- Teachers have the opportunity to make changes to classroom assessment, even if their school system does not.

- I propose a model of assessment that identifies the key processes and opportunities within the classroom whereby assessment can ensure that all learners improve their learning (figure 1f1).

In the following sections of this chapter, I shall consider the practical approaches of how to plan for formative assessment, develop meaningful learning objectives and outcomes, develop accessible success criteria and rubrics, review your questioning, deliver effective feedback and, finally, engage learners in peer assessment and self-assessment.

I start with the assumption that most teachers do most of these things to some extent. In each section, I will argue why I think its subject is an important aspect of classroom assessment, highlight the opportunities and pitfalls, and present suggestions of how to make improvements in your own practice. These improvements will be set in a context of a summative or formative culture of classroom teaching, learning and assessment.

2b) Towards a formative classroom culture

I'm privileged in my job to visit many schools, particularly within England, but also overseas, particularly in Kazakhstan. I am always astonished at the cultural differences between schools in the same region of England, but also amazed that I can step into a school in Kazakhstan and experience cultural similarities. In Chapter 1, I presented three pen portraits of teachers to illustrate the summative classroom culture, the formative classroom culture, and a mixture of the two. Culture is complex and is made up of, among other things, shared beliefs, attitudes and practices. Cultures endure through shared histories, experiences and behaviours. The culture of education, the idea that children need to be taught by their elders, is a pretty much universal human belief. However, culture is also localised within schools, communities, and even within a classroom. The teacher has a lot of influence in creating the learning culture of the classroom.

Your own pen portrait

With regard to assessment culture in schools, I have devised a brief, but, I hope, enlightening survey for thinking about the culture of your school and your classroom culture. It has been developed with a few groups of teachers as a basis for discussing classroom cultures, and is by no means perfect – I seem to make slight alterations each time I use it – but here it is in its current form.

To give an example of its use: a group of about 15 newly qualified teachers completed it during an after-school training session about assessment, data and progress. The group represented a variety of phases (early years, primary, secondary and special school) and subjects (English, maths, science, drama, history). Doing the self-report survey led to discussion about their views and the culture of their school. Some interesting points emerged. All said that they found the exercise useful and that the results were consistent with what they had anticipated. Several teachers felt their values were at odds with the expectations of their school; all of these wanted a more formative culture than school practices allowed. One teacher recognised that they brought different expectations to different year groups, teaching exam-year classes in a more summative way.

So, have a go at the short questionnaires, and then evaluate your responses using the reflection box at the end. Try not to agonise over each statement – go with your gut feeling.

Pen portrait 1: Your beliefs about assessment

First consider your beliefs: what you think assessment should be about. Read each statement and tick the box that best represents your views.

Table 2b1: Teacher beliefs questionnaire

Teacher beliefs	Strongly agree	Agree	Neither agree nor disagree	Disagree	Strongly disagree
The main purpose of school is to give learners the knowledge, understanding and skills they need to pass their exams.					
Examinations test the knowledge, understanding and skills that a child needs to be successful in life.					
The best teachers know how to get the best results in tests or exams.					
The best teachers have excellent subject knowledge.					
All learners have fixed ability that no amount of teaching can change.					
It is the teacher's responsibility to teach, and the learner's responsibility to learn.					
The main role of assessment is to let the teacher know how well a learner knows something.					
Test results give an accurate view of a child's knowledge, understanding and skills.					
The most accurate assessments are graded tests marked by external markers.					
Grades (as numbers or letters) are an accurate way of communicating the knowledge, understanding and skills of a learner.					
Total ticks					

Add up the number of ticks in each column, then move on to pen portrait 2.

Pen portrait 2: Your attitudes to assessment

This questionnaire is about your attitudes to assessment: what you think assessment should be like. Read each statement and tick the box that best represents your views.

Table 2b2: Teacher attitudes questionnaire

Teacher attitudes	Strongly agree	Agree	Neither agree nor disagree	Disagree	Strongly disagree
The teacher's only job is to teach the curriculum.					
The teacher is responsible for the grades their learners achieve.					
Once the teacher has taught something, it is the learners' responsibility to learn it.					
The teacher is responsible for their learners' learning.					
The best way to find out what learners know is to give them a test or marked assignment.					
Learners who often make mistakes in class are more likely to do badly in exams.					
Learners given low grades for their work will work harder to improve.					
Learners should have no involvement in assessment, apart from sitting the test/ assignment.					
Grades from tests or exams give me a reliable picture of a learner's knowledge, understanding and skills.					
Total ticks					

Add up the number of ticks in each column, then move on to pen portrait 3.

Pen portrait 3: Your practices and assessment

This questionnaire is about how teachers do assessment: what you do as assessment in your classroom. Read each statement and tick the box that best represents your views.

Table 2b3: Teacher practices questionnaire

Teacher practices	Strongly agree	Agree	Neither agree nor disagree	Disagree	Strongly disagree
Teachers teach everything that the students need for the final tests or exams.					
Teachers teach the curriculum in the time allocated by the timetable.					
Learners receive praise (or reward) for high marks or grades.					
Learners should work on their own assignment and not collaborate.					
Teachers' feedback on learners' work usually has a grade.					
The teacher is solely responsible for the assessment of learners' work.					
Learners are given regular tests, which are recorded and used for reporting.					
Learners get feedback in the form of grades only.					
Learners are not allowed to question the grade or mark given to their work.					
Total ticks					

Add up the number of ticks in each column, then move on to pen portrait 4.

Pen portrait 4: The assessment culture of your school

This questionnaire is about your school. What are the attitude, values and practices of your school regarding assessment? Read each statement and tick the box that best represents your views.

Table 2b4: School culture questionnaire

School culture	Strongly agree	Agree	Neither agree nor disagree	Disagree	Strongly disagree
The school is judged by the education system solely by the grades the learners achieve by the end of their schooling.					
The school is inspected by the education system on the grades that the learners achieve.					
Teachers are judged solely on how well their classes do in tests or assessments.					
Teachers are expected to teach the entire curriculum to all learners, regardless of ability.					
Targets for learners are based on target grades/ assessment alone.					
Extra-curricular activity is seen as less important than exam classes.					
Learners are considered to be of fixed ability and few change their position within their school career.					
Parents judge the school solely on the grades the learners get.					
Teachers are responsible for learners' grades so put on extra lessons and sessions to achieve this.					
High grades are rewarded more than high effort.					
Total ticks					

Add up the number of ticks in each column.

Transfer the totals of pen portraits 1–4 to 'Pen portrait: Summarising your results'.

Pen portrait: Summarising your results

Under each heading, transfer the results from your questionnaire. The charts are labelled to indicate the extent to which beliefs, attitudes and practices tend to be summative (towards the left) or formative (towards the right).

1 Teacher beliefs

Summative   *Formative*

Strongly agree	Agree	Neither agree nor disagree	Disagree	Strongly disagree

2 Teacher attitudes

Summative   *Formative*

Strongly agree	Agree	Neither agree nor disagree	Disagree	Strongly disagree

3 Teacher practices

Summative   *Formative*

Strongly agree	Agree	Neither agree nor disagree	Disagree	Strongly disagree

4 School culture

Summative   *Formative*

Strongly agree	Agree	Neither agree nor disagree	Disagree	Strongly disagree

Figure 2b1: Summarising self-survey results

Reflection

From the summary of your questionnaires:

- How do your beliefs, attitudes and practices compare? Can you explain this?
- How does your school culture compare with your classroom culture? Can you explain this?
- What opportunities are there for developing a more formative classroom culture?

Pen portrait of a newly qualified teacher 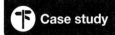 **Case study**

Josey is a newly qualified secondary school teacher of maths in England. Her pen portrait (figure 2b2) and analysis led her to realise that her attitudes were more formative than the school's. Teaching the 'core subject' maths, on which the school is judged, means that Josey and her classes are expected to meet targets of high attainment in tests. In terms of her assessment practices, Josey felt the school culture inhibited her from using more formative approaches, because the professional pressures on her – to get through the curriculum and ensure all her classes met the targets – were so great.

Josey summarised that she believed that creativity, making mistakes and the pastoral side of education were all important parts of mathematics education, but concluded the school's culture was 'by the book – and what the school wants, the school gets'.

1 Teacher beliefs

Summative   *Formative*

Strongly agree	Agree	Neither agree nor disagree	Disagree	Strongly disagree
	1	5	4	

2 Teacher attitudes

Summative   *Formative*

Strongly agree	Agree	Neither agree nor disagree	Disagree	Strongly disagree
		4	4	2

3 Teacher practices

Summative   *Formative*

Strongly agree	Agree	Neither agree nor disagree	Disagree	Strongly disagree
		5	5	

4 School culture

Summative   *Formative*

Strongly agree	Agree	Neither agree nor disagree	Disagree	Strongly disagree
2	5	3		

Figure 2b2: Case study: Pen portrait from Josey

Limitations of the survey

This survey is a basic one – it breaks down complex cultural aspects of education into just ten beliefs, attitudes and practices. Although this, in itself, is problematic, the purpose of the survey is, rather, to help teachers to reflect on their beliefs, attitudes and practices and consider these in the context of their school culture. This can then help them decide on the next steps for moving towards a more formative culture in their classroom, particularly if the school itself does not promote and support this.

2c) Planning meaningful assessment

My starting point when training teachers to plan their lessons is the insightful quote, 'People never plan to fail, only fail to plan'.[20] Most teachers, once established, spend less time planning as they get into a rhythm of teaching. They have lesson structures in their head that they can tactically draw upon to design and deliver a lesson. However, for those starting out in teaching, I am a great advocate of detailed planning of each lesson. This enables novice teachers to really think about, indeed visualise, their lesson before teaching it. Detailed planning promotes good habits, can be peer reviewed by a mentor before delivery and, all in all, gives the teacher a better chance of leading a successful lesson. Reading a lesson plan also gives me an insight into the teacher's thought processes, lesson structure, selection of resources, and considerations about the learners in that lesson. The more detail, the better understanding I have of that teacher's focus and approach.

I know that writing detailed lesson plans is not sustainable for every lesson on a full timetable, but even once you are an established teacher, interrogating your planning for a particular class or lesson can really help your professional development when you wish to make a change in your pedagogy.

If you are wanting to improve your classroom assessment, I suggest that an important first step is to review your lesson plan, be it a mental lesson plan or a written one.

In this section, we will explore how planning suitable learning activities, assessment activities and feedback activities can create a more formative culture.

---

[20]Attributed to Winston Churchill, a British Prime Minister, adapting a quote by Benjamin Franklin (a Founding Father of the United States).

Where planning for assessment fits in

Looking again at the classroom assessment model presented in Chapter 1 (figure 1f1), notice the relationship between learning objectives, learning outcomes and learning targets, superimposed by learning activities, assessment activities and feedback activities. These are all closely linked. The objective–outcome–target pillars are the foundations for planning a meaningful, formative lesson.

The labels added to the classroom assessment model in figure 2c1 show where the attention should be on learning, teaching and assessment, to move learners either towards the learning objective or beyond it. This section will provide a focus for each of these areas and consider techniques for teaching, learning and assessment to promote progress for every child. The techniques range from simple to more complex, yet in all cases, it's not what you do, but the way that you do it.

Creating a formative classroom culture through planning

Every action you take in the classroom is influenced by your underlying beliefs and attitudes. These practices are often implicitly shared with your learners; they become aware of what you value in teaching and learning.

To move from a more summative culture to a more formative culture in the classroom, a teacher will have to shift their practices to foster the values, attitudes and beliefs of a process-and learner-centred classroom. Through the explicit sharing of expectations and values, teachers and learners can create meaningful discussion, meaningful learning and meaningful assessment.

 Also see

This section introduces the main concepts relating to meaningful formative assessment. Next, you may wish to take a closer look at specific concepts in one of these sections:

- 2d) Questioning your questioning
- 2e) Developing meaningful objectives
- 2f) Developing meaningful success criteria and rubrics
- 2g) Giving meaningful and effective feedback
- 2h) Meaningful self- and peer assessment
- 2i) Using summative tests, formatively

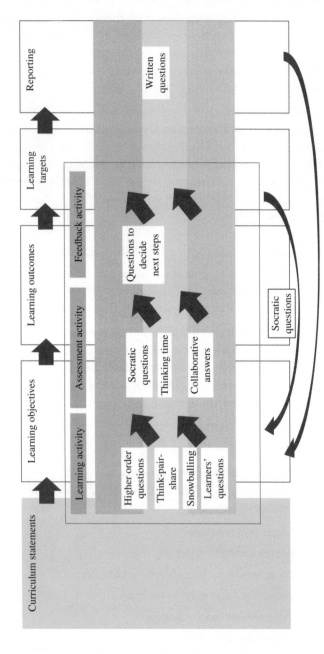

Figure 2c1: A model for classroom assessment: Planning meaningful assessment

How to plan for formative assessment: Bloom's taxonomy

The framework at the heart of all good educational assessment is Bloom's taxonomy.[21] I have used it extensively in teaching, assessment and curriculum design. However, there are some misconceptions and complexities that can hamper its use. Here, I describe what the taxonomy is, discuss potential issues, and show how it can be used effectively in the classroom.

The first thing to note is that there is 'old' Bloom's[22] and 'new' Bloom's[23] (revised in 2001). In the main, I will be discussing 'old' Bloom's, but 'new' Bloom's is explored in the research case study later in this section.

Bloom's taxonomy (abbreviated to Bloom's from now on) categorises verbs based on their cognitive demand – that is, the level of difficulty of the thinking skill required by the verb in question. For example, 'naming' an object requires knowledge, but not much thinking, but 'explaining' how something works requires knowledge and the ability to order that knowledge to explain an idea. Still more difficult is 'applying' knowledge to a new situation.

Bloom's is divided into three 'domains'. I see the cognitive domain dominate in schools, but the psychomotor and affective domains can inform higher order thinking in more physical and creative subjects.

Table 2c1: Cognitive domain categories of Bloom's taxonomy (2001) with example stem verbs, adapted by permission

Category (increasing demand)	Example stem verbs for use in assessment
Remembering	Recognise, recall, identify, retrieve
Understanding	Interpret, exemplify, classify, summarise, infer, compare, explain
Applying	Carry out (a familiar task), implement, use (a procedure)
Analysing	Differentiate, organise, attribute
Evaluating	Check, critique, detect, test, judge
Creating	Generate, hypothesise, plan, design, produce, construct

---

[21] **B.S. Bloom** (1956). *Taxonomy of Educational Objectives, Handbook I: Cognitive Domain.* New York: David McKay.

[22] **D.R. Krathwohl, B.S. Bloom & B.B. Masia** (1973). *Taxonomy of Educational Objectives, the Classification of Educational Goals. Handbook II: Affective Domain.* New York: David McKay.

[23] **L.W. Anderson, D.R. Krathwohl, P.W. Airasian, & B. Samuel** (2001). *A Taxonomy for Learning, Teaching, and Assessing: A Revision of Bloom's Taxonomy of Educational Objectives.* New York: Longman.

Bloom's can be used in many aspects of a classroom that values formative practices. It can be used for writing and communicating objectives and outcomes, planning questioning (both verbal and written), giving feedback, and target setting. Here I present some of the key features of Bloom's that are useful when planning classroom assessment.

The basic principles of Bloom's are that it is based on verbs that can be used for objectives and that some verbs are more challenging than others. Table 2c1 illustrates this. In the first column, categories for the domain illustrated are shown in order of increasing cognitive demand, from 'remembering' to 'creating'. In the second column, the 'stem' words are the verbs that start the assessment descriptor.

Imagine how this could be applied to a simple situation, for example the plot of *Star Wars: A New Hope*. You could apply Bloom's to set increasingly demanding questions:

- *Name* the main characters of the film.
- *Describe* the plot of the film.
- *Explain* why Luke didn't believe he was a Jedi.
- *Analyse* Darth Vader's actions throughout the film.
- *Evaluate* the role of the Jedi in the reclaim of the Empire.

Simplifications

I have often used simplifications of Bloom's when introducing it to trainees or teachers in workshops. My favourite is 'IDEAL': identify; describe; explain; analyse; link. However, this should just be a starting point, and the richness of Bloom's verbs should be regularly revisited.

Where and when to apply Bloom's

Bloom's can be used in planning and doing classroom assessment at all levels. It relies on the teacher understanding the current abilities of their learners and using Bloom's to ensure that the learners are challenged appropriately to make progress. So, the teacher can use Bloom's to design appropriate learning outcomes, plan verbal and written questions, decide upon suitable improvement targets, or feedback and communicate success with learners.

How to apply Bloom's

The most common way to apply Bloom's is to making learning outcomes differentiated, so that they are increasingly demanding. For example, in key stage 3 history, learning about the development of transport in England:[24]

- *Describe* how transport changed.
- *Explain* why railways were significant.
- *Analyse* the significance of the train by comparing it to other modes of transport.

Note that Bloom's cognitive domain works better for some subjects than others. In my experience, Bloom's cognitive domain works well for sciences and maths, history, geography and other humanities subjects. For languages (first and foreign), its usefulness is qualified, because the skills and concepts learned in those subjects are not always sequential. In art, drama and music, Bloom's affective or psychomotor domains may offer more useful stem words.

As with all frameworks, Bloom's has its limitations. When developing published schemes of work, I've faced the issues shared below.

Concrete and abstract concepts

Applying Bloom's to abstract concepts can be problematic. Abstract concepts such as energy, mental arithmetic and populations are more demanding than concrete concepts such as a particular fuel, using counters for arithmetic, or a single individual. Abstract concepts are usually difficult to see and require imagination to understand – that is, they require conceptualisation. The difficulty comes when a 'low' cognitive demand verb such as 'identify' is treated on an equal basis for concrete and abstract concepts.

For example, melting is a concrete concept in so far as a learner can see an ice cube melt. However, the particles that ice is made up of form an abstract concept. A learner needs imagination – a mental model – to understand why an ice cube melts or is the shape it is. So, using Bloom's, identifying that an ice cube is solid is concrete, but identifying the particle arrangement of a solid is abstract.

Stepping stones, access points, or pitch to the top?

An ongoing discussion among educational theorists and teacher educators is about how Bloom's should be used when planning learning outcomes. Should it be as stepping stones, where the common starting point is remembering verbs such as 'identify', and all learners move as far up the Bloom's categories as possible? Or maybe learners should access the verb most suited to their needs, so they are working at an appropriate level that stretches them? Or

---

[24] **A. Wilkes & K. Shearman** (2014). *Industry, Invention & Empire: Britain 1745–1901 Teacher Handbook*. Oxford: Oxford University Press.

indeed, could we start at the most challenging level and use the verbs below as support when learners need it? My preference is the second approach, where learners access the learning at different points, depending on their needs. However, there are arguments for all three. Try it and see.

What makes a question more challenging?

Here I share some aspects of Bloom's that have troubled me over the years and I have come to some clarity. I often see trainees treat the word 'define' as a word with a low level of cognitive demand. I often argue that define is actually a word with a high demand level, because it requires a fair amount of prior information, plus the ability to compare the idea or concept with other ideas and concepts. For a low-level objective I would favour a word that requires just knowledge recall, such as 'name', 'identify', or 'state'.

I also think we need to explain 'explain' a little further. There is a marked difference in the conceptual demand between explaining how and explaining why. Explaining *how* something happens usually requires a descriptive, recall-focused explanation. For example, 'explain how to make a cup of tea'. However, explaining *why* something happens is arguably more demanding, as other concepts need to be drawn together. For example, 'explain why Andy made a cup of tea' would require some understanding of purpose and cultural awareness. There are also differences in cognitive demand in multi-step explanations compared to single-step explanations, and in explaining something familiar versus something unfamiliar.

Creating and creativity

New Bloom's has 'creating' as the highest level, which many teachers seem to confuse with 'creativity'. In new Bloom's, creating is the ability to bring together diverse knowledge and understanding to create something new – the cognitive processes involved are 'generating, planning and producing', focused on hypothesising, designing and constructing. Creativity is an important concept in its own right and all learners should be encouraged to be creative, but this definition extends beyond Bloom's cognitive domain. My advice is to treat Bloom's' creating and creativity in education as separate concepts.

Different subject, different taxonomy

Bloom's cognitive domain is the go-to place for developing higher order thinking skills, but not all school subjects require the same skill set. The affective domain may offer some useful verbs for planning in the art subjects (table 2c2).

Table 2c2: Affective domain categories of Bloom's taxonomy (1973) with example stem verbs, adapted by permission

Category	Example stem verbs for use in assessment
Receiving phenomena	Acknowledge, ask, attend, being courteous, being dutiful, follow, give, listen, understand
Responds to phenomena	Answer, assist, aid, comply, conform, discuss, greet, help, label, perform, present, tell
Valuing	Appreciate, cherish, treasure, demonstrate, initiate, invite, join, justify, propose, respect, share
Organising	Compare, relate, synthesise
Internalising values	Act, discriminate, display, influence, modify, perform, qualify, question, revise, serve, solve, verify

Bloom's taxonomy

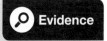 **Evidence**

Benjamin Bloom edited a framework of categories of educational objectives in 1956, which has since formed the foundation of assessment theory, teaching, learning, and the writing of examinations. Since I first became aware of what has become known as Bloom's taxonomy, I have used it in almost every aspect of my teaching and my ventures into assessment at all levels – classroom, school and policy. In an attempt to refocus and revitalise the original handbook, a team of authors reviewed the taxonomy and published a revised version in 2001. Here I summarise the key aspects relevant to classroom assessment, but I would recommend consulting this highly accessible revision. The points I highlight are relevant to many aspects of the rest of the book.

Anderson, L.W., Krathwohl, D.R., Airasian, P., Cruikshank, K., Mayer, R., Pintrich, P., Raths, J. & Wittrock, M. (2001). *A Taxonomy for Learning, Teaching and Assessing: A Revision of Bloom's Taxonomy.* New York: Longman Publishing.

In the new Bloom's, the authors have identified four major types of knowledge:

- *Factual knowledge*: the basic elements students must know to be acquainted with a discipline or solve problems

- *Conceptual knowledge*: the interrelationships among the basic elements within a larger structure that enable them to function together

- *Procedural knowledge*: how to do something; methods of enquiry; and criteria for using skills, algorithms, techniques and methods

- *Metacognitive knowledge*: knowledge of cognition in general, as well as awareness and knowledge of one's own cognition.

These four dimensions are then considered across the cognitive process dimension of: remember; understand; apply; analyse; evaluate; and create. The authors have produced a handy table and an abundance of examples of how to use it in a variety of contexts (table 2c3). This table can be used to identify different aspects of an assignment and compare the relative demand.

Table 2c3: The taxonomy table, cognitive process dimension, Bloom's taxonomy (2001). Reproduced by permission of Pearson.

The knowledge dimension	The cognitive process dimension					
	1. Remember	2. Understand	3. Apply	4. Analyse	5. Evaluate	6. Create
A. Factual knowledge						
B. Conceptual knowledge						
C. Procedural knowledge						
D. Metacognitive knowledge						

Phases towards planning for formative assessment

Figure 2c2 represents the suggested phases of planning for classroom assessment that moves towards fostering a formative assessment culture. Each phase is linked to the practices I discuss in the rest of this section.

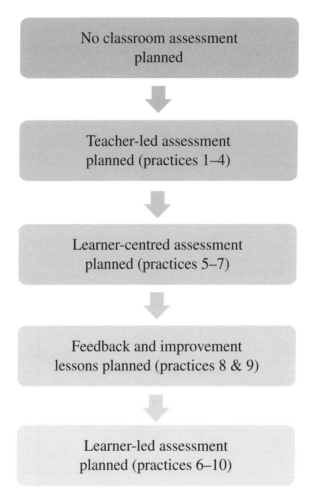

Figure 2c2: Towards lesson planning for a formative classroom

To help you establish which phase you are in and how to develop your practice, complete the 'practice analyser' questionnaire (table 2c4).

Practice analyser: Planning for classroom assessment

Read the statements, and for each one, tick the box that best illustrates your use of that practice.

To analyse your results, first identify the best-fit description for your practices. For example, are your responses mostly in the 'rarely' or 'never' categories? If so, you are likely to be in the 'no assessment planning' or 'teacher-led assessment planning' phases, so you would benefit from reading and applying practices 1–4 later in this section. But first, I give some more information on practices and potential next steps.

Table 2c4: Practice analyser: Planning for meaningful assessment

	Practice	Regularly	Often	Sometimes	Rarely	Never
1	I plan my lessons based on the curriculum requirements.					
2	I plan how I will assess learning within a lesson.					
3	I use learning objectives to structure the teaching and learning.					
4	I plan my questioning ahead of the lesson.					
5	I plan opportunities for learners to check how well they are doing during the lesson.					
6	I plan opportunities for self-assessment.					
7	I plan opportunities for peer assessment.					
8	I plan time for making improvements to work.					
9	I plan feedback opportunities in my lessons.					
10	My assessment in a lesson is used to inform planning of subsequent lessons.					

Analysing your practice and deciding your next steps

Once you have established the practices you use, decide which practice you would like to develop. Note that the practices at the top of the list are more likely to happen within a classroom with a summative assessment culture, and that they get progressively more likely to be found in a formative culture. Think about your school assessment culture and your own assessment beliefs and values so that you can make an achievable next step to improve your classroom assessment practice.

Mostly 'rarely'/'never'

If you do any verbal questioning at the moment, the next step is to try to identify some teacher-led assessment in your lessons (practices 1–4). This will help you understand where and when you assess and, if you don't, help you identify where and when you could identify assessment opportunities. Depending on the culture of your school and classroom, you may wish to start with practices 5–7. This will enable you and your learners to develop a more formative culture.

Mostly 'sometimes'

If you sometimes do most of these practices, choose one or two you would like to develop next. Carefully think about your school and classroom culture and consider which practices might benefit you in developing a more formative culture to improve teaching, learning and assessment in your lessons. Teachers in this situation may want to focus on improving just one practice, such as: planning your lessons so that they identify assessment opportunities more clearly (practice 2); planning opportunities for self- and peer assessments (practices 6 and 7); developing practices and opportunities for feedback and improvements to learners' work during the lesson (practices 8 and 9); or, more formally capturing evidence of learners' knowledge, understanding and skills to inform subsequent lessons (practice 10).

Mostly 'regularly'/'often'

If you have identified a practice that is 'sometimes', perhaps this is the one you may wish to develop, especially if it is lower down the table. If you are already using each of these practices regularly or often, perhaps you may want to evaluate how effectively you are using them. Reading one of the sections may help you analyse your implementation and give you new ideas to try and develop.

If you have fully established these practices, then look at another section of Chapter 2 to see what you might like to improve.

Note that the rest of this chapter looks at each of these strategies in more detail. This section on planning will consider the benefits of planning and consider some models of lesson plans and lesson structures. You will need to read the other sections for detailed descriptions of how to embed these strategies.

 Reflection

Decide on *one* area of practice that would help improve your planning of assessment in the classroom. Consider the constraints you have from your school culture and your own aspirations for a more formative classroom. Think what is achievable and what is likely to have the most success and impact on teaching, learning and assessment.

- Read the pages that relate to that practice or set of practices.

- Choose one class to trial the activities with.

- Reflect on how your practice has changed and the impact on teaching, learning and assessment.

Planning teacher-led assessment (practices 1–4)

Planning assessment within your lesson

Take a look at one of your recent lesson plans. What are the key features? Planning for assessment is often considered only in relation to the next test or assignment, with little recognition of the day-to-day assessment that occurs in the classroom. Most teachers use more assessment practices than they realise, even if they do not actually plan them.

The fact that lessons are based on curriculum requirements and, where appropriate, upon formal assessments such as examinations means that the teacher is planning by using the curriculum and associated assessment (practice 1). However, it is likely that there are several activities that such a teacher carries out without recognising that they are a form of classroom assessment.

Activities that are forms of classroom assessment, if used appropriately, include:

- establishing:

    - teacher-led questioning

    - learner-centred questioning

    - knowledge probes

    - students' prior knowledge, understanding and skills

- establishing where students need to be by:
  - sharing learning objectives and outcomes
  - sharing assessment criteria
  - finding opportunities to identify gaps and how to close them
  - finding opportunities to respond to feedback and make improvements
- establishing how to get there by:
  - providing suitable learning activities and resources to achieve targets
  - helping develop specific skills to achieve targets
  - providing appropriate scaffolding to support learning new concepts and skills
  - creating opportunities to look at exemplars or others' work
- establishing how far students have got by creating opportunities to:
  - check progress against objectives and outcomes
  - identify gaps and how to close them
  - respond to feedback and make improvements.

Most effective lessons have a beginning, middle and end. Often this is called the three-part lesson, composed of a starter, main activity and plenary. Alternative models do exist, often with additional stages, but the three-part lesson is fairly well established. This I have used as the basis of my examples.

A typical lesson plan includes what is going to be taught, and is usually divided into two columns: what the teacher will do and what the students will do. A third column to show assessment is less common. If your lesson plan lacks an assessment activities column, this is an easy first step to improving your classroom assessment – thinking about and identifying how assessment features in each part of your lesson and how that can improve learning.

Table 2c5 gives a generic lesson plan showing where and when assessment can take place. You may want to sketch a plan of your own lessons to identify where and when you do assessment (practice 2).

I will discuss the effective use of learning objectives and outcomes (practice 3) in more detail in section 2e. Here, what is relevant to planning is that objective-led lessons need to be planned and are an important part of creating a more formative culture. By way of illustration, table 2c6 shows

Table 2c5: Generic lesson plan illustrating assessment opportunities

Time	Teaching activity	Learner activity	Assessment activity
Starter	Provide starter activity that can assess prior knowledge against learning objectives.	Attempt the starter activity.	Teacher circulates, checking, prompting and questioning.
	End of activity: teacher asks each group to provide answers.	Learners provide their answers to the teacher verbally.	Teacher assesses prior knowledge and shares this with learners.
	Teacher shares learning objectives and expected outcomes.	Learners engage with learning outcomes and establish what is expected of them.	Teacher checks that learners understand what is expected of them.
			Learners question teacher if they need clarification.
Main	Teacher introduces main activity.		
	Teacher gives instructions, reminds class of how long they have to complete the task, and checks they know what to do.	Learners attempt task.	Teacher circulates, using planned key questions to probe and extend learners while doing the task.
			Teacher identifies misconceptions and challenges them with the individuals or, if necessary, the whole class.
Plenary	Teacher leads a short question-and-answer session using planned questions.	Learners answer questions.	
	Teacher gives learners five minutes to review their work against the success criteria.	Learners self-assess their work.	To ensure key ideas are understood, teacher circulates to support learners with self-assessment, prompting and guiding. Establishes what they understand, how well they understand it and what needs more work.

how the lesson objectives, along with learning outcomes, can be shared, and lead the learners through what is to be learned and how well it can be learned during a lesson.

In this generic example, table 2c6 shows how teaching, learning and assessment activities can be planned so that the learning objectives are met in a lesson with two learning objectives, each with three learning outcomes defined:

- objective 1
  - outcome 1A
  - outcome 1B
  - outcome 1C
- objective 2
  - outcome 2A
  - outcome 2B
  - outcome 2C

There are a variety of strategies that can be used to achieve this. Throughout this book, I describe a number of activities that are suitable – in the meantime, they are presented as generic teaching, learning and assessment activities.

Table 2c6: Example generic plan for assessing objectives and outcomes

Time	Teaching activity	Learner activity	Assessment activity
Starter	Starter activity	Learners explore and share what they know already.	Establishes prior knowledge of objectives 1 and 2
Main	Activity 1 facilitates learning for knowledge and understanding of objective 1.	Learners construct knowledge and understanding of objective 1.	Teacher and learners assess against outcomes 1A, 1B and 1C.
	Activity 2 facilitates learning for knowledge and understanding of objective 2.	Learners construct knowledge and understanding of objective 2.	Teacher and learners assess against outcomes 2A, 2B and 2C.
Plenary	Plenary activity reviews knowledge, understanding and skills of objectives 1 and 2.	Learners can identify what they have done well and where they can still improve.	Assess against outcomes to identify success and next steps (e.g. 'I achieved 1B and 2A. Next time I need to achieve 1C and 2B by...').

The underlying assumptions are that teaching and learning take place informed and guided by assessment strategies. Both the teacher and the learners know how well the learning objectives are being addressed. Note also that the teacher is using teaching activities that *facilitate* learning and these activities, in turn, allow learners to *construct* their knowledge, understanding and skills associated with the learning objectives. The teacher can keep track of how well the learning is going by referring regularly to the learning outcomes; if shared with the learners, they themselves know what they are aiming for.

The final part of the lesson, the plenary, allows the teacher and students to assess how well each of the objectives has been met and identify next steps in teaching and learning.

Planning your questioning (practice 4)

Questioning is often overlooked as an important part of planning assessment in the classroom. It is also sometimes practised ineffectively, as discussed in section 2d. For now, just consider how questioning can be planned for a lesson. On a lesson plan there are variety of ways to plan your questions; here I will explore just three of the key aspects for you to consider.

Planning questions that foster more formative values

Instead of focusing on how many items learners got right, on the outcomes of tasks, and whether or not they can perform a particular skill, you can change your language to shift the expectation from 'get everything right' to 'learn, make mistakes, strive to make improvements'. Here are some questions a teacher with a more formative classroom culture may ask:

- What did you get wrong? Do you know why you got it wrong?

- What do you need to do to improve? How could you make that improvement?

- What have you learned by doing this?

- What did you do to be able to achieve that?

- What do you still need to do to master that task or skill?

- What have you learned from others in this lesson?

- Have you made progress? How do you know?

Notice how the language focuses on learning, progress and improvement. It allows those mistakes and values the time taken to correct them, as well as opportunities for learners to learn from each other.

Planning key questions

Each lesson will have key concepts or skills to cover. Identify the key questions you will want to ask the whole class or individuals during the lesson, perhaps linked to specific activities.

A primary school lesson about how to use a dictionary 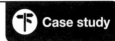 **Case study**

The teacher has set a task for the learners to look up the meanings of various words using a dictionary. The objectives were based on the purpose of the dictionary, how words are organised within a dictionary, and how definitions are presented. The teacher has key questions she has planned to use to ensure that each learner can meet the lesson objectives:

- Why do we use a dictionary to find the meanings of words?

- How are the words arranged in the dictionary?

- What do the different definitions mean?

- And an extra 'stretch question' – what else could the dictionary be used for?

Having planned these key questions, the teacher does not need to think of questions in high-pressure lesson time, is aware of the key questions that relate to the lesson objectives, and is able to draw on these questions at every opportunity.

Planning learner-centred assessment (practices 5–7)

One of the key features of a more formative classroom culture is giving learners more involvement in the assessment process. The types of practices that foster this culture include planning opportunities for learners to check their own learning, self-assessment and peer assessment – practices 5, 6 and 7 respectively. Relatively simple changes can be planned to shift the focus on summative assessment values to formative assessment values. The following classroom case study illustrates this.

Planning student-centred assessment

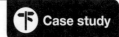 **Case study**

I recently observed a science lesson in which Coz, a trainee teacher, gave out worksheets where the 11–12-year-old learners were expected to fill in gaps in sentences with the correct key words and label the diagrams. The lesson was about the structure and function of the human reproductive systems. After they had completed the worksheets, Coz went through the answer to each question. When discussing the lesson Coz identified that the process of 'going through each answer' took too long and the learners became restless and bored. We then discussed an alternative: reviewing the task using a self-assessment activity.

In the fifteen minutes it took to go through the answers on the worksheet, Coz came to realise that if he had provided the learners with an answer sheet and got them to mark their own, they would have been engaged in self-assessment. If then he turned his interest from what they got right to what they got wrong, the values of the lesson would shift from outcomes to processes of learning – from summative to formative values. So, an alternative approach would be to give the class five minutes to mark their own answers, correct any answers they got wrong, and identify any areas they still didn't understand. Coz then could spend five minutes questioning, focusing on what the learners got wrong. Questions could include: 'Which questions did you get wrong?'; 'Why?'; 'How might you mention that in the future?'; and 'Is there anything you still don't understand?'.

These questions would reveal that some learners were confusing the words 'urethra' and 'ureter'. There would be opportunities to share ways of remembering the difference. In the same way, organs that are common to male and female reproductive systems and those that are different could be discussed.

This case study shows that just a simple change in lesson structure and questioning can shift the values from summative to more formative. This short episode within the lesson allows learners to work out what they know, where they are stuck, and remedy the situation. If used regularly, small changes in practice can create a more formative culture.

In this case it was an exercise of self-assessment, but it could easily be peer assessment. Both of these practices involve developing routines, trust, and common expectations – these are explored fully in section 2h. Both provide unique opportunities for learning, and both put the learners at the heart of the assessment process, so that learning can take place.

Planning opportunities for feedback and improvements (practices 8 and 9)

As I will demonstrate in section 2g, effective feedback seems to be key to effective learning and has been increasingly understood to be *the* way to achieve the best gains in learning. Planning opportunities for giving effective feedback and opportunities for learners to respond to that feedback are significant in improving learning.

A more formative culture moves values from outcomes to processes, where the feedback and improvement aspects of learning are valued through the practices of the teacher. If opportunities for feedback and improvement are planned in the lesson, learners will see that the teacher values these activities. So, plan time both for making improvements (practice 8) and for effective feedback opportunities (practice 9).

In order to make time for and value time for review, assessment and improvement in the lesson, teachers have to reconsider the structure of their lessons. These can be simple changes (as with Coz's shift in the previous case study) from teacher-led marking to learner-led self-assessment, or can be wholesale shifts in lesson plans. Three example lesson structures are illustrated in figure 2c3.

Example 1 shows the standard three-part lesson, and is a representation of 'the beginning, the middle and the end' of the story of a lesson. In example 2, a lesson structure that values formative assessment and improvement is shown. Here, the first part of the lesson is devoted to learning about and drafting a task. In the second part, the draft is reviewed against the criteria. The rest of

Example 1

Starter	Main	Plenary

Example 2

Drafting	Reviewing	Improving

Example 3

Teacher assessment	Reviewing	Improving	Self-assessment or peer assessment

Figure 2c3: Lesson structures towards a formative culture the lesson is focused on developing the task, based on the improvements that came up in the review section of the lesson.

An example of shifting the onus of learning to the learners – example 3 – demonstrates how, after learners do a project that is assessed by the teacher, a lesson of improvements is planned, based on what the learners need to do next. In the next classroom case study, I describe one such lesson that I have taught.

Example of planning opportunities for improvements

Case study

The class of 14-year-olds had used a rubric that I had designed to complete a small project on household energy efficiency. They had to produce a customer leaflet that set out the advantages and disadvantages of various methods of energy saving and demonstrated how much money each method could save the customer over a year.

I collected the projects and marked them using the success criteria on the rubric. I put a tick next to criteria met and a 'T' (for target) next to the criteria that were the next steps. This method of marking revealed that there were four main areas that the class needed to improve on: calculating payback times; understanding the different ways heat is transferred from a house; how insulating materials work; and how double glazing works to reduce heat loss. Using this information, I devised four activities for the lesson. Each one was based on improving knowledge and understanding of these areas. The activities were simple:

- Use pages 12–14 in the textbook to find out about calculating payback times.

- Write instructions for how to calculate payback times.

- Calculate the payback times of the energy-saving methods that you got wrong or did not complete.

When the learners arrived for my lesson, I handed back their work and described what they had done well, then explained what they needed to improve and how. They were set the task to attempt two targets during the lesson, using the resources provided. Throughout the lesson, I circulated amongst the learners as they attempted their improvement tasks. I could help them when they had questions, needed direction, or felt they had completed a task. They variously needed clarification of expectations, guidance on where to find information, or just encouragement to have a go at something they were finding difficult. After half an hour, the learners were asked to assess whether they had improved their knowledge, understanding or skills in their target areas by using the rubric.

This case study is an example of lesson structure 3 in figure 2c3. The shift from a focus on outcome to one on improvement made the lesson culture more formative. As a teacher I was valuing not the marks or grades, but what students were learning, making improvements on, and the problems they were tackling. Therefore, the learners were making effort to improve their work, asked for help when struggling, and felt more independent when trying to solve problems.

Planning lessons based on meaningful assessment (practice 10)

There are various ways to plan lessons based on prior assessment information. Many teachers do this tacitly between lessons. They are able to know 'how far the class got', 'how well they understood it', and make decisions on whether to do some more work on a particular area in the next lesson. It is hard, however, to capture assessment information from all the learners in a single lesson. Among the successful strategies that can be used to remedy this, an 'exit ticket' is a simple approach with numerous variations.

The exit ticket  Case study

Exit tickets are often a slip of paper that learners complete at the end of the lesson before they leave. They take various forms, some generic and some specific to the lesson. In all cases they encourage learners to reflect on what they have learned and identify areas they need further work on. In a lesson I observed, Lily, a secondary geography teacher, had prepared a slip of paper like the one shown.

Lily had a stock of these slips of paper to use regularly in lessons. At the end of the lesson, each learner was expected to complete the ticket and hand it to Lily before they left the lesson. The lesson had been about different types of land form caused by rivers and the 13–14-year-olds had been given a variety of information sources such as textbooks, a short video, some photographs and an online animation. As the class filed out, each learner handed Lily their exit ticket. A couple of learners, Lily noticed, had not fully completed the slip, and she made them go back to their desks to finish it before allowing them to leave.

Exit ticket

What I learned this session:

What I already knew:

What I might need some more help with:

How I feel about this session:

Figure 2c4: Example exit ticket

Lily then read the tickets and sorted them into piles – a process that took about five minutes. She was able to get an objective view of what her class had learned, what they needed more help with, and how they felt about the lesson. Most learners had learned that rivers shape the landscape, which was the main objective of the lesson. The types of things that the learners said they needed more help with allowed Lily to plan her next lesson:

> *I can see that most of them learned about waterfalls and plunge pools, but most of them didn't get as far as oxbow lakes. They seemed to enjoy the lesson – this one says, 'I liked the videos, they made it easy to understand', and another 'I enjoyed drawing the diagrams of the waterfall'. So this approach is working for them. I can continue with this approach for the next lesson, but need to spend a bit more time on the formation of lakes before we go on to looking at our local river. Oh look, this one asks about how our local river has formed the town. We will be covering that later.*

Lily used the exit tickets to check which objectives had been met, how well they had been met, and what further work could be done. This she used to modify her plans for next lesson to ensure all learners understood the formation of lakes before applying the ideas to the local river. I liked the last question on the ticket because it also gave Lily an insight into how well her teaching approach was working.

Variations on the exit ticket

Some teachers state the lesson objectives and ask the learners to rate how confident they feel about each one. In contrast, I like to know how well the class have done, so I am more inclined simply to ask, 'What have you learned this lesson?' and 'What would you like to know more about?' as this forces the learner to consider what they have learned, rather than just giving a rating. Learners are often keen to get out of a lesson quickly, and will rush or even try to avoid doing the exit ticket. As you saw, Lily forced a couple of learners to go back and finish theirs. Ensure that enough time is given at the end of the lesson to enable the task to be valued, and completed thoughtfully.

At the end of a lesson where learners have been creating something, the question 'if you had five minutes more, what would you have done?' can create some interesting information to explore in the next lesson. This is sometimes used in music lessons where learners are composing, or in drama when they are creating a sketch.

Using test results to inform lesson planning

In section 2i, I will explore this in more detail, but to summarise: if a test is taken, ensure that an analysis of the results is used to inform, at a minimum, your subsequent teaching and, ideally, the learning of each individual that has taken that test.

Longer-term planning for assessment

This chapter has focused on short-term planning – a lesson-by-lesson approach. This is deliberate, because I am writing the book from the perspective of helping teachers to question their assessment approach and make small, achievable changes. Once teachers have found techniques that they find useable, I would recommend that they then start to think on a longer-term basis and plan whole topics or year-long programmes of study that take on board these approaches.

 How to

To plan for meaningful classroom assessment, make sure your lesson plan includes:

- a section for learning objectives and success criteria
- columns for teaching activity, learning activity, and assessment activity
- planned questions and questioning strategies that address the learning objectives
- planned assessment that allows teacher and learner review and feedback on progress
- planned use of assessment information to decide next steps in learning
- planned lesson structures that allow review, self-assessment, peer assessment, and opportunities to improve.

2d) Questioning your questioning

This section considers how teachers can develop their practice of questioning in the classroom, and focuses on verbal questioning. When 'questioning your questioning', you should consider the culture of your school and your classroom, as well as the beliefs and attitudes that need to be cultivated in order to make your practices effective.

Where questioning fits in

Some questioning techniques are more effective than others at promoting formative assessment values. Figure 2d1 shows where in a teaching episode effective questioning can be used, and indicates some techniques.

 Also see

This section builds on section 2c) Planning meaningful assessment.

It also has direct application to:

- 2e) Developing meaningful objectives
- 2g) Giving meaningful and effective feedback

The culture of teachers and questioning

Questioning is deeply engrained in the culture of teaching. It is accepted that teachers ask questions and can answer their learners' questions. This has historical foundations in both Western and Eastern philosophies. Socrates, the ancient Greek philosopher, is often heralded as the father of teaching in Western cultures, to the point that Socratic questioning is still used in schools and colleges, and there remains a research interest in the practice.

The idea of learning through questioning is at the heart of this philosophy. Some see it as a craft, but I see it as a skill that can be developed over time and through experience. There is a skill to asking the right question at the right time for a particular learner. It is a complex skill that requires the teacher to know what makes an effective question, distinguish different types of question, and understand the learner, in order to judge the most effective question to use at a particular time.

While working in China I read about Confucius, who I considered to be the philosophical equivalent to Socrates in Western cultures. Multi-talented, he was a philosopher, politician and teacher, among other things. China's

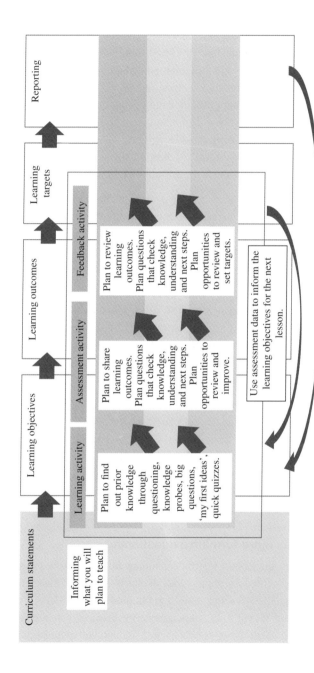

Figure 2d1: A model for classroom assessment: Using questions for assessment

Confucian heritage is at the heart of Chinese society: children in Chinese schools learn about his thinking.

Kazakhstan is of particular interest culturally, because it has a history of Soviet rule, becoming independent in 1990[25]. Since then, the country has been in the process of developing its own education system. However, the authoritarian Soviet influences in education remain. As one Kazakh teacher told me when we were talking about culture and questions: 'I think in Kazakhstan we still have the Soviet Union influence to some extent, where a dictating, authoritarian regime was held by authority. The structure of society was different, too. That is why I think teachers mostly asked closed questions – just to check whether they [the learners] know or do not know something.'

Not only do learners feel the effects of a more authoritarian educational culture, the teachers do too. Great strides are being made to give teachers more freedom in their teaching – many of my Kazakh colleagues are doing just that – but it is slow progress, as Soviet values persist, and the Kazakh political system is still more authoritarian than democratic.

Despite questioning being part of our cultural fabric in education, it can often be reduced to a performance, with the teacher as the 'sage on the stage' asking questions and encouraging students to answer. The skills are too often underdeveloped: the teacher asks questions because that is what teachers do, not because they have any deep understanding of why they are asking questions and how best to ask those questions.

When I am training new teachers, it is often questioning that they find challenging. As far as I am aware, both Socrates and Confucius taught one-to-one or small groups, not large classes of thirty or more. Not only does whole-class questioning require the skills of questioning, it also requires the skills of classroom management – yet another layer of complexity. Reflecting on my experience, questioning is the skill that I have continually developed through my career and am unlikely ever to perfect.

Phases towards more formative questioning

The model I have developed for understanding approaches to classroom questioning is presented in figure 2d2. It starts with an absence: 'no verbal questioning'. The teacher takes a traditional, didactic role; owning the knowledge and giving it to the learner. The learners just receive the knowledge; their understanding is not checked through verbal questioning. If

---

[25] **C. Robbins** (2008). *In Search of Kazakhstan: The Land that Disappeared.* London: Profile Books.

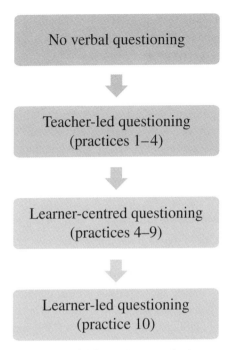

Figure 2d2: Towards meaningful formative questioning

this is your style, then introducing some teacher-led questioning techniques could be employed to improve assessment.

Teacher-led questioning is what is traditionally seen in classrooms, with the teacher at the front. They ask a question, some learners raise their hands, and the teacher selects one of the them to reply. The teacher evaluates the answer and may praise or reprimand, then puts another related question to the class. And so the cycle continues. This technique can be very problematic, as I will illustrate below, but with some refinement and practice can be effective for some types of learning and assessment.

Learner-centred questioning techniques allow more formative values to be developed. These can be more effective in finding out what learners know, and can, if done with care, allow learning to take place through the questioning. There are pitfalls in these methods too, and the values of a formative approach need to be at the foundation of the successful planning and deployment of these strategies.

Finally, shifting the responsibility from the teacher to the *learners asking questions* to probe and develop knowledge, understanding and skills can be achieved through various techniques. These can be valuable to both teacher and learner in a number of contexts. This, however, is the most challenging approach, as most classrooms do not have a culture that allows this to be easily achieved.

Let me first highlight some aspects of questioning that are problematic. These feature in classroom research in Western countries, but I have also experienced them in some classrooms in Kazakhstan. It is important to recognise that most teachers fall into these traps from time to time. However, being aware of the problems and how to remedy them really can help improve your questioning.

Questioning your questioning

I think it is important to establish the purpose of questioning in the context of assessment. The main purpose of questions in the classroom should be to: assess knowledge, understanding and skills (including prior learning); check knowledge, understanding and skills before moving on; and help develop knowledge, understanding and skills. This section will help you to understand why you are asking questions, and establish if it is the most effective way of assessing the knowledge, understanding and skills of your learners.

Educational research into classroom questioning has been substantial, with a concentration of studies in the 1980s and 1990s[26], particularly based in Western countries.[27] This established research base means that we have a good idea of how questioning is carried out in classrooms and the implications of different questioning practices for educational outcomes.

The traditional method of questioning, with the teacher initiating the question, the learners responding and the teacher feeding back has been given a variety of names, but most often the Initiate–Respond–Follow-up (IRF) model or the triadic dialogue. For example:

Teacher (initiates question): What is the tilt of the Earth's axis?

Learner (response): 23.5 degrees.

Teacher (follow-up): Correct, good answer.

There are many problems with this method if it is not done well. Even when done well, there are, arguably, more effective ways to achieve the same purpose. Let's consider the main pitfalls.

---

[26] **J.L. Lemke** (1990). *Talking Science: Language, Learning and Values*. London: Ablex.

[27] **J. Wellington & J. Osborne** (2001). *Language and Literacy in Science Education*. London: McGraw-Hill Education.

One or all?

In classrooms where there are many learners, it takes a very skilled teacher to include all of them in a questioning session. I often observe teachers asking questions where just a few students put up their hands and answer questions. Those learners get the question right and the teacher moves on with another question. This approach assumes that if one learner knows the answer, then all the learners in the class know the answer. It also assumes that a learner must be confident that they know the answer to put their hand up (and if no one puts their hand up, the teacher assumes that no one knows). My favourite description of this scenario is that, with the teacher often asking the same few learners to respond, the rest become 'sleepy onlookers'.[28] In a large class, it is difficult to assume that all the learners are fully engaged and learning from the answers of their peers.

Guess what's in my head

The next pitfall is the type of questions asked. Questions can be described as closed or open. Closed questions require brief answers – a single word or short phrase. Open questions require a more in-depth, thoughtful answer.

Examples of closed questions:

- What is the capital of France?
- What is the boiling point of water?
- What is four multiplied by four?

At worst, closed questions can lead to a game of 'Guess what's in my head', as this example illustrates:

> What was the name of the instrument we heard last lesson?... Yes, Johnny?... No, it was made of brass... Jamilia, remember?... No, not a triangle, but it begins with 'T'... No, Spencer, not a trumpet... bigger than a trumpet... Claire?... A trombone? Close. Micha?... Not a flute, that doesn't begin with 'T'... It was a tuba... a tuba.

I still sometimes find myself at a point where my questions are getting like this. So, I stop myself, tell the class the answer, and move to a more useful questioning approach.

Closed questions are often knowledge-checking ones; rarely do they reveal understanding. In addition, they have a single right answer. This reaffirms a summative culture, where the teacher leads the learning and assessment and

---

[28]**P. Black, C. Harrison, C. Lee, B. Marshall & D. Wiliam (2003)**. *Assessment for Learning: Putting it into Practice*. Maidenhead: Open University Press, p. 98.

the outcome is more valued than the process. A tip for opening up closed questions is to add the question, 'Why?' Try it for the previous examples – they certainly become more challenging.

Open questions

Open questions, on the other hand, can offer opportunities to foster a learning-focused, process-valuing culture. Learners have more options in how to respond; they are required to think more deeply about their answer; and are challenged to give more than a one-word answer.

Open questions usually have more than one answer, require application of prior knowledge, and should challenge learners. For example:

- Why do you think that the earthquake happened here?

- How do think this rock formation came to be like this?

- What do you think Romeo was thinking when he found Juliet?

These questions all require thinking and expect the learners to make some suggestions. When they provide an answer, it is worth asking them to justify their answer, give a reason or support it with evidence. This type of questioning requires some shared understanding of the values within your classroom and your expectations, so you will need to develop this way of working with your learners.

 Reflection

Thinking about teacher-led questioning:

- To what extent do you use the IRF method in your lessons?

- How often do you plan your questioning? Do you see any benefits it would have?

- Which pitfalls of questioning have you encountered? How do you usually deal with them?

- How could you avoid these pitfalls in future?

Developing your questioning

Now you have questioned your questioning and I have explored some of the problems with classroom verbal questions, have a go at evaluating your own practice. In the following questionnaire (table 2d1), decide how often you do these practices with a particular class.

Table 2d1: Practice analyser: Towards meaningful formative questioning

	Practice	Regularly	Often	Sometimes	Rarely	Never
1	I lead the questions in the lesson.					
2	I plan my questioning ahead of the lesson.					
3	I use questions to check understanding.					
4	I feel confident in dealing with wrong answers.					
5	I feel confident in answering learners' questions.					
6	I use questioning approaches that involve all the learners.					
7	Questions are used to decide next steps in a lesson.					
8	I use methods that increase thinking time.					
9	I allow learners to collaborate before answering questions.					
10	My learners lead the question-and-answer sessions.					

To analyse your results, first identify the best-fit description for your practices. For example, are your responses mostly in the 'rarely' or 'never' categories? If so, you are likely to be in the 'no verbal questioning' or 'teacher-led questioning' phase, and would benefit from reading and applying practices 1–4 later in this section. But first, here is some more information on practices and potential next steps.

Analysing your practice and deciding your next steps

Having established the practices you use, decide which practice you would like to develop. Note that the practices at the top of the list are more likely to happen within a classroom with a summative assessment culture, and they get progressively more likely to be found in a formative culture.

Think about your school assessment culture and your own assessment beliefs and values so that you can make an achievable next step to improve your classroom assessment practice.

Mostly 'rarely'/'never'

If you do any verbal questioning at the moment, the next step is to try some teacher-led questioning (practices 1–3). This will help you gain confidence in planning effective teacher-led questioning. The learners will also go through a shift in understanding your expectations and the benefits of being questioned in this way. However, depending on the culture of your school and classroom, you may wish to start with practices 6–9. This will enable you and your learners to develop a more formative culture.

Mostly 'sometimes'

If you sometimes do most of these practices, choose one or two you would like to develop next. Carefully think about your school and classroom culture and consider which practices might benefit you in developing a more formative culture and improve teaching, learning and assessment in your lessons. You may want to focus on improving just one practice, such as planning questioning to be more learner-centred and formative (practice 2), dealing with wrong answers (4), developing practices that include all learners (6), questions to decide the next steps in the lesson (7), or strategies to increase thinking time (8).

Mostly 'regularly'/'often'

In the case of mostly 'regularly'/'often' answers, if you have identified a practice that is 'sometimes', perhaps this is the one you may wish to develop, especially if it is lower down the table. If you are already using each of these practices, you may want to evaluate how effectively you are using them. Reading one of the sections may help you analyse your implementation and give you new ideas to try and develop.

If you have fully established these practices, then look at another section of Chapter 2 to see what you might like to improve.

Reflection

Decide on *one* area of practice that would help improve your questioning in the classroom. Consider the constraints you have from your school culture and your own aspirations for a more formative classroom. Think what is achievable and what is likely to have the most success and impact on teaching, learning and assessment.

- Read the pages that relate to that practice or set of practices.

- Choose one class to trial the activities with.

- Reflect on how your practice has changed and the impact on teaching, learning and assessment.

- Think about your school assessment culture and your own assessment beliefs and values so that you can make an achievable next step to improve your classroom assessment practice.

Developing shared values in questioning (practices 1–10)

Moving questioning from a teacher-dominated, outcome-focused activity requires a shift to a shared understanding of the purpose of questioning. Learners need to be aware of the rules, the reasons and the benefits.

A good place to start when establishing a more learner-centred questioning strategy is to establish ground rules with the class. The class will be more responsive if they understand why they are answering questions and why you are doing this part of the lesson. For example, share with the learners that you wish to ask some questions to help them understand a particular concept. Explain to them your expectations:

- I am going to ask you some questions and I want you to do your best to answer.

- Even if you are not asked to answer, I want you to be thinking of your answer.

- Don't worry if you are not certain of your answer: have a guess.

- By the end of the questions session, I want you all to have learned something new.

To instil these values, make sure you praise when students have a go at an answer. Ensure that you focus on the process of learning and not on the outcomes of correct answers. When students give an answer, tell them why it is a good answer. Find the positive. And then ask another question to take it further. For example:

Olga: I think it is due to the volcano.

Teacher: Good, you have given me an answer; why do you think that?

Olga: Because we learned about volcanoes last lesson.

Teacher: Okay, so do you think volcanoes and earthquakes are linked?

Olga: Not sure…

Teacher: That's fine, let's think it through together. Does anyone else think that volcanoes and earthquakes are linked?

Classroom questioning

I have selected this research paper as an example of a relatively recent study into classroom questioning. It is based in an Eastern culture, and uses a sociocultural perspective. Although it focuses on just two teachers, the study reveals a deep, rich analysis of how classroom questioning can be improved. Also note that these research findings can be, with caution, applied across all subjects in all countries.

Chin, C. (2006). Classroom interaction in science: Teacher questioning and feedback to students' responses. *International Journal of Science Education*, 28 (11), 1315–1346.

The study was carried out in Singapore in secondary science lessons (12–13-year-olds). It draws on data from seven one-hour lessons from two teachers. The classes were considered to be of average-to-high ability, and there were about forty students in each class. The lessons were recorded on audio or video and the transcripts analysed, using detailed coding.

The aims of the study were to:

- develop an analytical framework that represents classroom talk and questioning in science

- find out how teachers use questioning to engage their students in thinking about conceptual content that enables the construction of knowledge, and

- identify the various forms of feedback provided by teachers in the follow-up move of the IRF format of teaching exchange.

The study found that teachers can promote productive talk beyond recall by:

- avoiding explicit evaluation or put-downs

- acknowledging learners' contributions

- posing subsequent questions that build on learners' responses.

The author concludes (p. 1343):

Students can be stretched mentally through sensitive teacher-led but not teacher-dominated discourse. As orchestrators of classroom discourse in shaping students' learning, teachers need to position themselves as enablers of talk for thinking. One way of doing this is to pay particular attention to the follow-up move of the pervasive IRF exchanges in teacher–student talk, and consciously pose a series of meaningfully related questions that stimulate students to tap into higher-order thinking processes.

Developing teacher-led questioning (practices 1–4)

In a classroom culture dominated by summative assessment, the next steps to improvement could be to improve the quality of teacher-led questioning. This can start to establish some practices and values that move towards a more formative culture. The first suggestion is to plan your questioning; the next explores how to increase involvement of more learners in questions; and the final one how to increase thinking time. If you haven't already, look at the research case study, which shows the types of responses that foster learning.

Planning your questions

Unplanned questioning can often default to low-level, closed questions, which fill time, but do not add anything to learning or assessment. By planning questions as part of their lesson plan, a teacher can feel more confident in asking meaningful and suitably challenging questions.

You could use Bloom's taxonomy (see section 2c) to increase demand when checking prior knowledge. For example, in a science lesson using a microscope, questions before starting the practical could be:

- What is the microscope used for? (*Know*)

- How do we use a microscope safely? (*Describe*)

- How does the microscope work? (*Explain*)

- If you can't see the specimen through the eyepiece, what actions could you take? (*Apply*)

An added sophistication would be to identify the learners who will be challenged by each question, and direct the questions at them. This is often known as targeted questioning.

In the same lesson, there will be questions to check key knowledge and understanding while the teacher circulates and helps students. Such questions can be written down as a prompt for the teacher and focus for learners:

- What is that part (of the microscope) called? (*Know*)

- What does it do? (*Explain*)

- What can you see? (*Describe*)

- Which parts of the cell can you see? (*Apply*)

- What is the function of the nucleus/cell membrane/cytoplasm? (*Describe* and *Explain*)

Reflecting on your questions

After each questioning session, reflect on its effectiveness. Ask yourself if you kept to your questions, how the learners responded, the effectiveness of the questions, and what you would do next time. Making a written note is useful, but even a mental note is helpful for the next occasion.

Moving from teacher-led to learner-centred questioning (practices 4–9)

This stage is about taking on more of the values and practices of a formative classroom. Throughout this book, I argue for a shift in the involvement in learning and assessment to the learner. These practices can begin to foster and reinforce more formative values. In a strongly summative culture, teachers and learners will have beliefs and assumptions about questioning that include the role of the teacher initiating and leading the questioning and judging the answers. The learners will value recognition for knowing the right answers – the outcome of learning, but not its process.

Creating a safe learning culture

Moving from a teacher-led to a learner-centred classroom culture requires a change in roles, expectations and responsibilities. With regard to questioning, the teacher still plans the questions, but will focus through questioning on the process of the learning, not on its outcome. The teacher can achieve this by sharing their intention with their learners, offering the opportunity to try something new, and reflecting with them on the experience of the process.

Dealing with wrong answers (practice 4)

Using questioning strategies that are more formative means that there are more opportunities for learners to get answers wrong. This is good, because they are learning. However, in a summative culture, getting answers wrong is not valued and can make learners lose confidence or face ridicule. In a summative culture, teachers are often dismissive of wrong answers – either not challenging them, or just moving to someone else. In a formative culture, there are more positive ways to engage with the wrong answer and make a learning point from it, thus reinforcing the value of the learning process.

Answering learners' questions (practice 5)

Shifting the control of questions from the teacher to the learners also opens up concerns for the teacher with respect to answering learners' questions. Some teachers believe their role is to be a 'fount of knowledge'; others, a 'facilitator' for learning. In a more learner-centred approach, the latter role allows the teacher to recognise that it is their role to guide a learner to an answer, rather than tell them. I had a head of department who only answered questions with another question. The learners enjoyed the challenge of this, but found it frustrating if they were just asking to visit the toilet. Taking this further, Socratic questioning is a legitimate and usable approach to questioning more focused on the learner and learning.

Socratic questioning

So far, the questioning approaches we have considered are based on checking knowledge and understanding, mostly for the benefit of the teacher. However, questioning itself can facilitate learning to take place. Socratic methods are employed to do just that. These methods are still applied and are the focus of educational research, bringing insights into how children learn through questions. This type of questioning does require practice and skill to develop.

The set of beliefs that underlie the Socratic methods include the idea that all thoughts can be developed through more questions – that learners can learn when guided by the teacher through appropriate questioning. Linda Elder and Richard Paul summarise the practices of a teacher using Socratic questioning, where the teacher:

- responds to all answers with a further question to develop the thinking of the learner
- seeks to uncover the ultimate foundations of learners and follow the implications of these foundations through further questions

- encourages learners to find connections between their thoughts

- explores and raises prior questions.[29]

Categorisation of Socratic questions has been attempted by several practitioners. In table 2d2 I present a version of the types of Socratic question and examples of questions the teacher may ask. This is a useful template on which to hinge your ideas.

With this type of questioning, the challenges of teaching large classes still remain. Teachers have to consider the purpose of using this style of question. Plan to use it when it will be most effective. Using it at the start or end of a topic allows a teacher to probe and develop knowledge and understanding of individuals and the class. Perhaps a follow-up activity can help focus all learners on the questioning session. Tell them at the start that they will be expected to write a summary of their learning at the end of the questioning session. Then give them five minutes to write their response to the original question.

Table 2d2: Six types of Socratic question: a starting point

1 Clarification	What are you trying to achieve in saying this?
	What is your main aim in this line of thinking?
2 Probing assumptions	What information are you basing that comment on?
	How do we know this information is accurate?
	How did you reach that conclusion?
3 Probing reasons or evidence	Could you explain your reasoning?
	What evidence are you using? Why?
4 Viewpoints and perspectives	What alternative explanations are there?
	From what perspective are you looking at this?
	Is there another point of view you can consider?
5 Implications and consequences	What are you implying when you say that?
	How does that relate to...?
	What would happen if...?
6 Questions about questions	What is the main idea you are putting forward?
	Can you explain that idea?
	Can you clarify that point for me?

[29] **R. Paul & L. Elder** (2007). Critical thinking: The art of Socratic questioning. *Journal of Developmental Education*, 31(1), 36.

Involving all learners in questioning (practice 6)

One of the main challenges of questioning a whole class is how to involve all learners. There are number of techniques to shift the responsibility from the teacher to the learner. Here, I explore one of those strategies.

'No hands' rule

In order to encourage whole-class engagement, the teacher specifies that learners should not raise their hand to offer an answer. Instead, the teacher will ask a learner at random (or select one) to give an answer.

This strategy straddles teacher-led and learner-focused questioning and is probably a good approach to develop in the first instance of making this transition. The strategy does require some additional considerations so that learners feel confident to be involved (and the teacher has skills to deal sensitively with wrong answers). This is discussed in the following section.

Deciding the next steps in learning from questions (practice 7)

If you plan your questions effectively, ensuring that they reveal knowledge and understanding of the learning objectives (see section 2c, practices 1–4), then the answers that learners give can reveal the next steps in learning. The questions can be used to establish prior knowledge and understanding of new knowledge or concepts. Look at this section's classroom case studies to see how the teacher finds out what the learners know and how they use this to inform next steps.

Increasing thinking time (practice 8)

A number of studies have shown that in the traditional IRF model of questioning, most teachers expect an answer in less than a second. This leads to unnecessary pressure and, consequently, low-quality answers. Sometimes the type of answer is clearly wrong, because the learner hasn't had time to think. For example, if I ask you 'What do cows drink?' your first thought, or even answer, may be 'milk'. This is clearly the wrong answer, unless you are thinking of a calf, but it shows how short thinking time can cause poor-quality answers. To avoid this, strategies can be used to increase thinking time between the question and answer. This has been shown to increase the quality of answers.

The benefits of increased thinking time are that learners will respond with richer, more thoughtful and useful answers. It means that the teacher will need to ask fewer questions. Thinking time is also called 'wait time' (if you are researching this further). I prefer the term 'thinking time' because it is focused on the learner, not the teacher.

There are various strategies teachers can use, but all share these underlying principles:

- The question has a clear purpose.

- The question is challenging.

- The question is open.

- The learners have time to think, either on their own or with another learner, before offering an answer.

So, a simple change in practice could be that you tell your learners that you are going to ask them a question, or write it, or display it on the board, and you will give them a full minute to think about their answer. After one minute, ask a few learners at random for their answers. Bring together the key points and assess what they know and which areas will need more development.

Think–pair–share (practices 8 and 9)

A more effective method could be introduced where learners discuss their answers with the learner next to them. Giving them time to share and compare their ideas improves confidence and motivation to use the thinking time allocated. This is often called the think–pair–share method.

Snowballing

This is an extension of the think–pair–share method. After pairs have discussed and decided on their best answer, they join a nearby pair of learners and compare answers. Based on this discussion, learners write down what they consider to be the best answer. Finally, the snowball gains another layer: two groups of four share their answers and decide their best answer. This can be done in a total of three minutes – one minute for each stage. In turn, one learner from each group of eight presents their best answer, which means that the teacher will be able to assess the knowledge, understanding and skills of the class from hearing a small number of responses.

Developing routines

Learners will take time to get used to new approaches to classroom questioning, but with expectations shared and regular use of the approach in small doses, they will soon become more familiar, comfortable and confident in the approach. Some guidelines:

- Share the rules of the strategy.

- Explain the purpose.

- Describe what success looks like.

- Reinforce the responses that you want to value.

- Reflect on the process with the learners.

- Repeat to establish the routines.

Snowballing

 **Case study**

On the interactive whiteboard, Simon displays the rules of 'snowballing' questioning to his class of 11–12-year-olds. He explains that its purpose is to create the best answer they possibly can to the question he will ask shortly. Simon states that he wants the learners to learn from each other and together create the most complete and accurate answer they can. Referring to the instructions on the board, Simon explains the procedure. He tells them that once they hear the question, they will have 30 seconds to write down their first attempt, on their own. Then they will have one minute to share, compare and improve their answer with the person next to them. There will be another minute in two pairs, sharing, comparing and improving their answer, and finally, in a group of eight, 90 seconds to follow the same process and come up with an agreed best answer. Each stage requires the learners to write their notes on paper. Simon displays a timer and explains that it is important that they work fast.

The learners are poised with their pen hovering over their first piece of paper. Simon reveals the question: 'How does a sunflower seed become a sunflower?' Timing each section, Simon circulates, encouraging learners to write down their own ideas, then share, compare and improve.

Once the final snowball layer is completed, Simon has three 'best possible answers'. They are mostly written, but one group has also drawn a seed and sunflower with labels and arrows to show what goes in (e.g. sunlight) and comes out (e.g. oxygen).

Simon displays the three responses at the front of the class and congratulates the class on their teamwork and their ability to think and improve their work. He then asks one learner from each group to state what they learned from the process and to explain why they think their answer is good.

Case study commentary

First note how long the actual activity took. It was four minutes, plus three minutes of teacher-led discussion. Most standard question-and-answer sessions last from five to ten minutes and rarely include all students. Simon explains the rules clearly and makes his expectations clear, highlighting what he values in the process; he is establishing a formative approach to questioning. The question itself is open and has a focus based on the topic. Simon has selected it to establish prior knowledge and understanding of the class. He can see the key words they know, how they use those words, and the limits of their knowledge. Two of three responses used the word photosynthesis (in various spellings); all the responses conveyed that sunlight was involved; one group thought, incorrectly, that the plant 'ate' the soil. Simon can base his planning on this information, spending more time on areas of difficulty and less time on what learners already know. Notice also that Simon's final questions are about the learning process and confidence in the response presented. This emphasises the value of the learning process over the final outcome, thereby reinforcing formative values.

Moving from teacher-led to student-led questioning (practice 10)

With emphasis on control of the questions moving from teacher to learners, the teacher is able to assess knowledge, understanding and skills from the questions the learners ask. For many classrooms this is a significant culture shift, with different responsibilities and roles for both the teacher and the learners. The pressures on the teacher change – to managing the volume of learner questions, ensuring that all questions are addressed, and making sure that all learners are involved.

The advantages of this approach are learners' increased sense of ownership of the knowledge taught and learned within the classroom and thus increased motivation and interest in the topic. Having a vested interest in the topics being studied will help achieve greater learning outcomes within the lessons and throughout the topic. By referring back to the learner who asked the question as each question is addressed, the teacher builds a sense of joint discovery.

This approach can be set, at the start of a new topic, by asking the learners what questions they would like answered about the subject. The following classroom case study exemplifies this approach.

Learner-led questioning

 **Case study**

At the start of a topic on ancient Egypt, primary school teacher Matthew puts a question to his class of 9–10-year-olds: 'What would you like to know about the ancient Egyptians?' He asks them to write down three questions. Each question could be written on a separate piece of paper or sticky note. Questions from the class included:

- Who were they?
- What was it like in ancient Egypt?
- How long ago were they around?
- Who were all their gods?
- Do mummies really come to life?
- How did they live without electricity?
- How did they build the pyramids?
- Do the pyramids still exist?
- Did they get eaten by crocodiles?

Matthew collects the questions and sorts them into different categories, many of which match the curriculum. Some questions are general, others specific. What Matthew can see immediately is that some of the learners know very little about ancient Egypt. Others know a small amount, and there are some misconceptions. Matthew makes use of this information in planning his lessons, and uses different learners' questions as the starting points for each session. This makes the lessons learner centred – still covering the curriculum, but starting from learners' own questions and prior knowledge.

A note on written questions

This section has focused on verbal questioning – on moving from teacher-led verbal questioning to learner-focused questioning and on to learner-led questioning. Based on what you have learned about verbal questioning, you could also consider how you might improve the written questions you use to help learners test their knowledge and understanding.

Reflection

Think about how you might plan and use formative questioning. Consider moving from teacher-led questions to learner-centred questions:

- Plan approaches that link your questions to specific learning outcomes.

- Plan questions that increase in demand, suitable for the subject you are teaching.

- Find opportunities to use focused questions in a variety of classroom situations.

- Reinforce your expectations through explicitly sharing them verbally and putting them into practice.

- Prepare, practise and reflect on learner-centred questioning to ensure learning opportunities for all learners during a questioning session.

2e) Developing meaningful objectives

Creating a formative classroom culture through meaningful objectives

We rarely go to a meeting without receiving an agenda – we need to know at least what the meeting will be about and what it hopes to achieve. In the same way, if learners know what the lesson is about and what they should achieve during that lesson, they have a far better chance of being successful.

This section considers the first three columns of the classroom assessment model (figure 1f1): the bridge between the curriculum and what is taught and learned in the classroom. As a teacher, your job is to translate the curriculum statements into learning objectives. In this section's title I use the term 'meaningful' because, as a class, learners need to have shared meaning of what they need to achieve. If they understand the goal, they have a better chance of success. I will also illustrate how objectives can be meaningless and written only for the benefit of school leaders, rather than the learners.

The purpose of objectives

When I get a phone call from someone who is lost and in need of directions, the first thing I ascertain is where they are now. Then I explain their next steps for getting to where they need to be. We need to keep this in mind when we are teaching. Objectives must be challenging, but realistic. The purpose of learning objectives is to develop a shared understanding of what we are trying to achieve in a lesson or learning episode.

Consider the example of this section of the book. With regard to its purpose, I could do any of the following:

1 not tell you what to expect, just let it emerge as you read

2 share what I expect you to do, in a question such as: 'How do you use learning objectives and outcomes for classroom assessment?'

3 be more specific about what you will know, understand and be able to do after reading the section: 'By the end of the section you should: (a) have read the section; (b) know how to use learning objectives; (c) know how to write and use learning objectives in your teaching; (d) be able to reflect on your own classroom assessment practices; (e) be able to explain the benefits of using objectives to lead teaching and learning.'

The first two examples are quite common approaches in traditional lessons, but they have the assumption that the learner will just receive and absorb the information passively, with no agency in learning the material. If you know what you are trying to achieve by the end of the section, it is more likely that you will focus on that. The third approach is task orientated and achievable. Moreover, it has a focus on what I want you to 'know' by the end (example learning objectives (b) and (c)). 'Know' as a verb isn't easily measurable, though, whereas objectives (d) and (e) require you to be able to 'reflect' and 'explain'. Both these objectives are specific, and I would be able to assess how well you can reflect and explain.

Objectives and outcomes

There is often confusion over the purpose of objectives and outcomes, and even what the terms mean. Yet having precise learning objectives and realistic but challenging outcomes is imperative to a formative culture.

To illustrate the distinction between objectives and outcomes: if you split a class into two groups and give each group an envelope containing the instruction: 'List as many uses of a brick that you can. You have ten minutes', but with an addition for group 2: 'List a minimum of 20 uses', I guarantee that group 2 will get a longer list. Group 1, lacking a target, will think they have done well to find about twelve uses. Group 2, however, will push themselves to come up with more ideas. In this situation, the objective is clear for both groups. For group 2, the desired outcome is also specified, resulting in improved performance. Knowing the purpose of the lesson and what you are trying to achieve can be the difference between success and failure.

Some clarifications

Before going on, it is important to get some clarity on the language used here. Many terms are used to describe learning objectives and learning outcomes. These include – but are not limited to – aims, goals, outcomes, success criteria, and targets. While there is often confusion when I work with English-speaking colleagues, when I have taught through translators in Russian, Kazakh and Chinese, there is even more, particularly in Russian, where the translated words for objective and outcome are the same. I was running a workshop in Kazakhstan when I came up against this issue. The good thing about working with translators is that there is time to think between the sentence just spoken and the next. Having learned that in Russian there is a single word for objective and outcome, I found the following phraseology helpful: '*What* we are going to learn' and '*How well* we will aim to learn it'. Since then, I have used this as my default when working with trainees, authors and teachers. I don't mind what the concepts are called, so long as they have these two functions.

Table 2e1: Characteristics of learning objectives and learning outcomes

What we are learning? (Learning objectives)	How well? (Learning outcomes)
A statement of what should be learned, not done, in a lesson.	Look at the curriculum or the examination specifications for stem words.
Should be challenging.	Definitely should be measurable.
Should be measurable?	Should be increasingly challenging.
Avoid 'know', 'understand', 'become familiar with'.	
Only 1–3 per lesson.	

Formulating learning objectives

A concern among some teachers is that learning objectives (what we will learn) will 'give away' the answer at the start of the lesson. They complain that it takes away the surprise of the lesson, or the opportunity for their students to find out for themselves.

There's a commonly used science lesson that involves measuring the mass of a length of magnesium, burning it, and measuring again. The purpose of the lesson is to demonstrate the concept of conservation of mass: when magnesium burns, the product left has a greater mass because it has reacted with oxygen in the air. A 'give-it-away' objective would be: 'By the end of the lesson you will be able to explain why the mass of magnesium increases when burned'. A better objective could be: 'Investigate and explain the effect of burning on the mass of magnesium.'

Furthermore, effective learning objectives should focus attention on the development of knowledge, understanding or skills, not the activities to be completed in the lesson. For example, 'Write an essay about the causes of World War I' or 'Paint a still life' are objectives merely focused on the lesson activities, rather than what will be learned. Meaningful objectives need to be carefully considered to promote learning, self-evaluation and self-regulation. Writing effective objectives for lessons is something I have found takes a lot of practice, and does require trial and error.

Characteristics of meaningful learning objectives

These:

- link to the curriculum

- focus on learning of knowledge, understanding or skills

- are challenging, but achievable

- use language that is accessible to learners

- inform the teaching and learning activities of the lesson

- allow assessment of learners' progress in the lesson.

We can relate all these characteristics to this section's research case study about the importance of encouraging self-efficacy. How the teacher creates objectives, introduces them and engages learners with them is critical in developing a formative culture. What teachers say and do, and when they say and do specific things, will influence their learners' engagement, motivation, and ultimately, independence through self-regulation.

Where meaningful objectives fit in

Learning objectives need to be planned, based on the curriculum statements, and designed to be accessible and meaningful to teachers and learners. Figure 2e1 shows how well-designed learning objectives link to learning outcomes and, if they have not yet been achieved, eventually become learning targets. This section looks at how learning intentions can be shared, and how learners can engage with them and make meaning. Learning outcomes, or success criteria, are then dealt with more extensively in section 2f.

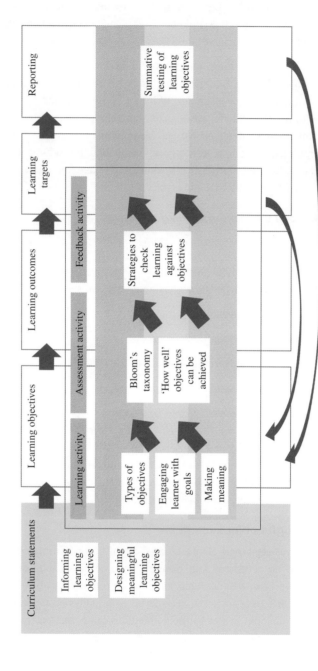

Figure 2e1: A model for classroom assessment: Meaningful objectives

Phases towards developing meaningful objectives and outcomes

Figure 2e2 represents the suggested phases in making lesson objectives effective for fostering a formative assessment culture. Each phase is linked to the practices I will discuss in the rest of this section.

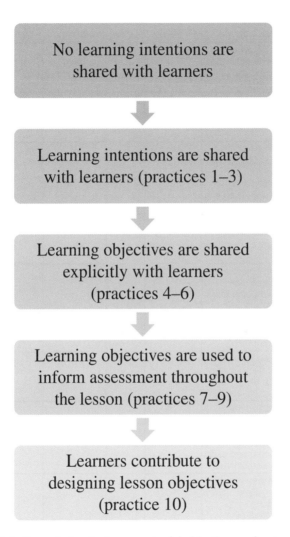

Figure 2e2: Towards developing meaningful objectives and outcomes

To help you establish which phase you are in and how to develop your practice, use the following questionnaire.

Practice analyser: Developing meaningful objectives and outcomes

Go through the questionnaire (table 2e2) and, for each statement, tick the box that best illustrates your use of that practice.

Table 2e2: Practice analyser: Towards meaningful objectives and outcomes

	Practice	Regularly	Often	Sometimes	Rarely	Never
1	My lessons start with a title or question, so that my learners know what they are doing.					
2	I write and share a list of tasks for my learners so they know what they should do.					
3	I write and share statements that identify the knowledge, understanding and skills the learners will learn in a lesson or during a topic.					
4	My learners write down the objectives and outcomes at the start of every lesson.					
5	My learning objectives and outcomes use Bloom's taxonomy stem words (or similar).					
6	My learning outcomes are linked to a grading system.					
7	I use a rubric to communicate success criteria with my learners.					
8	The last part of my lesson allows learners to check their knowledge, understanding and skills against the objectives.					
9	During the lesson learners regularly check their learning against the learning outcomes and make improvements to meet the objectives.					
10	I work with my learners to create our own objectives and outcomes for a lesson or topic.					

Also see

This section builds on 2c) Planning meaningful assessment.

It also underpins:

- 2d) Questioning your questioning
- 2f) Developing meaningful success criteria and rubrics
- 2g) Giving meaningful and effective feedback
- 2h) Meaningful self- and peer assessment

To analyse your results, first identify the best-fit description for your practices. For example, are your responses mostly in the 'rarely' or 'never' categories? If so, you are likely to be in the 'no assessment planning' or 'teacher-led assessment planning' phases, so you would benefit from reading and applying practices 1–4 later in this section. But first, here is some more information on practices and potential next steps.

Analysing your practice and deciding your next steps

Having established the practices you use, decide which practice you would like to develop. Note that the practices at the top of the list are more likely to happen within a classroom with a summative culture, and they get progressively more likely to happen in a formative one.

Think about your school assessment culture and your own assessment beliefs and values so that you can make an achievable next step to improve your classroom assessment practice.

Mostly 'rarely'/'never'

If you do share what is going to be the focus of the lesson as a title or question, you may want to consider how to develop meaningful learning objectives and outcomes (practices 1–4). This will help you understand a range of approaches and construct a shared understanding of them with learners, enabling you and your learners to develop a more formative culture.

Mostly 'sometimes'

If you sometimes do most of these practices, choose one or two you would like to develop next. Carefully think about your school and classroom culture and consider which practices might benefit you in developing a more formative culture and improve teaching, learning and assessment in your lessons. You may want to focus on improving just one practice – maybe one about creating and sharing meaningful learning objectives (practices 4–6), or weaving learning objectives into the whole lesson to encourage self-reflection and self-assessment (practices 7–9), or trialling ways in which to involve your learners in creating meaningful learning objectives and outcomes (practice 10).

Mostly 'regularly'/'often'

In the case of mostly 'regularly'/'often' answers; if you have identified a practice that is 'sometimes', perhaps this is the one you may wish to develop, especially if it is lower down the table. Next, if you are already using each of these practices, you may want to evaluate how effectively you are using them. Reading one of the sections may help you analyse your implementation and give you new ideas to try and develop.

If you have fully established these practices, then look at another section of Chapter 2 to see what you might like to develop.

 Reflection

Decide on *one* area of practice relating to effective learning objectives that would help improve your classroom assessment. Consider the constraints you have from your school culture and your own aspirations for a more formative classroom. Think what is achievable and what is likely to have the most success and impact on teaching, learning and assessment.

- Read the pages that relate to that practice or set of practices.
- Choose one class to trial the activities with.
- Reflect on how your practice has changed and the impact on teaching, learning and assessment.

Using titles and questions (practice 1)

Traditionally, lessons start with titles. The first thing I remember doing in any lesson is to write the date and the title. Usually, the title indicates the content of the lesson. The title is normally displayed by the teacher and learners dutifully write it down. It could be a word or phrase that is familiar, or a word or phrase the learners have never heard of. Although this practice focuses the lesson on a specific set of knowledge, the underlying assumptions are that the teacher owns the knowledge and is giving it to the learners. The learners have no engagement with the topic beyond copying it down.

In a formative culture, we want to foster learner involvement with the entire learning and assessment process – not only the title of the lesson, but what they should be learning, and ideally, what that learning looks like.

Questions are an alternative way to present titles with which to share learning intentions – 'What were the main causes and effects of the Irish potato famine?', 'Which conditions can make a reaction go faster?'. Questions are more engaging than titles, because they at least encourage the learners to think about learning. Questions create a moment for learners to reflect on whether they know the answer, or can at least respond to the question in some way.

Open questions are better than closed questions (see section 2d), as they allow more than one answer or a more in-depth one. This technique works well if the question is revisited at the end of a lesson so learners can reflect on what they have learned.

Questions at least engage learners in what they are learning about, but do not communicate much more than that. The next step would be to create more meaningful learning objectives, which indicate not just *what* to learn, but *how well* it should be learned. This is discussed in practice 3.

A list of lesson tasks is shared with learners (practice 2)

Some teachers use titles or questions to share intentions (practice 1), together with a list of activities or tasks for the class to carry out to meet these intentions: 'Copy figure 1 and label it', 'Answer questions 1–10 in full sentences', and so on. This gives learners a clear agenda to meet the lesson intentions. The hope is that by doing these tasks they will learn the content of the lesson. This is a traditional system, where the knowledge is given to the learners and learned in an identical format. I can imagine the exercise books looking very similar, with the focus on the work being correct, and no space for making mistakes. Such learners are in an outcome-focused culture, rather than a process-focused, formative one.

Some tweaks to this approach could shift this traditional approach to a more formative one – for example, providing options for learning about a specific topic. In practice 1 we considered shifting from a title to a question. The question could then be addressed via a number of options.

In my view, these are objectives without meaning. Although learners now know what to do, they do not know what to learn or how well to learn it. The list of tasks focuses on the outcomes, rather than the process of learning.

It is much easier to focus on processes if the learning is made explicit: this is discussed in practice 3.

Learning intentions are shared with learners (practice 3)

Learning intentions focus on what is to be learned, not what is to be done. There is often more than one way to learn something, and, in some cases, learners can be given a choice of activities or open-ended activities to learn the same knowledge, understanding or skills.

What is important here is to be explicit about what learners should learn, not what they should do. The assumption is that the lesson is focused on learning, not doing. With this expectation, learners can focus on what they are learning.

When learning intentions are shared, they need to be accessible to the learners. So the language needs to be considered carefully, so that learners can understand exactly what it is that they are meant to be doing. For example, Julia, a primary school teacher in England, shared with me some learning intentions used for maths lessons. Julia varies the language used according to the age of the children. The language is important in helping create meaning, and the more carefully language is used, the more likely it is that the teacher and the learners will have a shared understanding. This is explored further in practices 5–7.

Learning intentions in primary maths 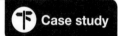 Case study

Julia showed me her learning intentions for two classes. Designed for a term of teaching, just one or two are covered in a lesson or week of learning maths.

Years 1 and 2 (aged 5–7)

Let's learn to…

- count in 2s, 5s and 10s

- use addition and subtraction to problem solve

- read, write and interpret mathematical statements involving addition (+), subtraction (-), and equals (=) signs

- partition numbers in different ways

- add and subtract one-digit and two-digit numbers to 20.

This is a useful illustration of type of language and purpose of learning intentions. The learning intentions for years 1 and 2 are clearly focused on learning. They are informed by the national curriculum for England, but have been made more accessible to the learners. By using 'let's learn to...' terminology with the class ('Let's learn to count in twos'), the teacher gives a sense of learning together, constructing ideas together, and being part of the learning process.

Year 5 (aged 9–10)

- Find percentages of amounts and quantities.

- Use equivalence with fractions to find percentages.

- Work systematically through problems and explain reasoning.

- Solve problems involving decimals.

- Compare numbers with up to three decimal places.

- Practise adding and subtracting decimals mentally.

For year 5, the teacher's language changes, but is more specific about the skill required. For example, the verbs, 'find, solve and compare' are very specific skills required for learning that knowledge, understanding or skill. In fact, the year 5 learning intentions are beginning to be learning objectives (practice 4).

Learning objectives are shared explicitly with learners (practice 4)

In practice 3, I defined learning intentions as statements of what is to be learned in the lesson, rather than what is to be done. The shift was from a list of activities that may result in learning to the process of learning the knowledge, understanding and skills expected in the lesson. We now move to the practice of using learning objectives. These are different because not only do learning objectives share what is to be learned, they also indicate how well it should be learned.

Engaging learners with learning objectives

To make learning objectives meaningful, both teacher and learner should develop a shared understanding. If a teacher is going to use objectives effectively, they need to form the thread of a lesson within the overall content.

Various illustrations of this were described in section 2c, when considering how to plan for classroom assessment. This goes beyond just stating the objectives orally, having them written on the board, or both.

Objectives without meaning

When I was involved with a whole-school approach to improving assessment for learning, something we focused on was the effective use of objectives. To establish how objectives were written and being used across the subjects, we randomly sampled lesson objectives from around the school.

The main findings were interesting. As usual, the context is important. The school had a policy that teachers were expected to write objectives on the board, so that they were shared with the learners. This was monitored by senior management 'dropping in' on lessons unexpectedly. As a result of this, an array of different forms of learning objectives were displayed (often lists of tasks or questions), but frequently the teacher and learners did not engage with them at all. These pseudo-objectives were, basically, just an elongated version of a title. However, in the best cases, the learning objectives were carefully constructed; learners engaged with them, and the learning objectives formed the thread throughout the lesson. Every learning activity was linked to the learning objective, the shared goal was plain to see, and success was clear. Again, it's not what you do; it's the way that you do it.

How to share learning objectives

Learning objectives should be embedded in a learning episode, within the long term (where they fit in an academic year), medium term (where they fit within a topic) and short term (where they fit into a lesson).

I would argue there is no set method for sharing learning objectives, but that useful strategies have these characteristics:

- Learning objectives are focused on learning, not doing.

- They are accessible and understandable to learners.

- They are shared verbally and in writing.

- They are discussed, to develop a shared understanding.

- Key words within the objectives are discussed if they are new or unfamiliar.

- A model of what success looks like is provided.

Learning objectives are shared explicitly with learners (practice 5)

A method championed by many who use formative assessment employs Bloom's taxonomy. In this section, I will assume that you have read section 2c, which explains 'Bloom's'. The verbs provided by the taxonomy provide a sense of the cognitive demand of an objective. The expected outcome is defined beyond what is to be learned, by encompassing the extent to which it should be learned.

In sharing such objectives with your learners, it is essential to make explicit the meanings of these verbs and what they may look like – for example, the difference between 'describe' and 'explain', or 'compare' and 'analyse'. This is often best achieved with exemplars or models. The first few lessons will devote more time to this, but as learners become accustomed to it, the process will increasingly become more of a reminder than an in-depth discussion.

It is important, if you are starting this approach, to realise that you can learn with your learners – discuss with them to develop a shared meaning of the Bloom's verbs. You will find your understanding deepens and your approach evolves with experience.

Ana, a languages teacher in England, shared with me some learning objectives for Spanish revision for a class of 14–15-year-olds:

- To understand content of year 10 exam

- To practise verbs

- To practise writing skills

- To understand how to revise.

Here, the class knows what is expected and, in most cases, the teacher can discuss the objectives to check the learners are on course to succeed. Note that the objectives are focused on 'doing' – such as practising verbs and writing skills – and they quite general; for example, 'to understand'. The next step is to think about how the learning objectives could be written to be more meaningful – that is, to focus on learning and be specific about exactly what the learning looks like. This is discussed in practice 6.

Learning objectives are shared explicitly with learners (practice 6)

You may have realised that I haven't spoken much about using grades in classroom assessment. This is because there is significant research to show that the use of grades in communicating assessment with learners has detrimental effects on learning, progress and achievement (see section 2i). However, most countries are stuck with a system that depends on grades – in fact, so heavily reliant on grades that they are part of the educational culture. Indeed, most of the learning ladders I have written have been grade-linked in some way, either explicitly, as in the level ladders,[30] or implicitly, as with 'establishing, secure, extending' rubrics.[31]

In an ideal world, grades would not be the only guide for assessment, but we have a system that requires it, and many learners, teachers and schools are focused on grades. To navigate this when doing classroom assessment, ensure that grades have shared meaning. If the teacher and the learner have a common understanding of a 'grade A' or 'grade C' then learners will make more sense of the learning goals. Many exam boards produce assessment criteria for some or all of the grades; these can be useful for pitching each learning objective to the appropriate level.

However, caution is needed because in an exam system that is based on ranking students (normative), a criteria-based approach can limit potential if it is used to the letter. Instead, learners aiming for an A grade must aim for at least that criterion, and take opportunities to exceed it, in order to ensure success in a norm-referenced system.

Looking for assessment clues in grade descriptors

An example is for Modern Foreign Languages (MFL) at GCSE level in England, where the government has published grade descriptors for grades 8, 5 and 2.[32] The grading system is 9 (the highest) to 1 (the lowest). In the 'writing' assessment domain:

> To achieve grade 8 candidates will be able to: write effectively for different purposes explaining ideas, expressing and justifying opinions and manipulating vocabulary and grammar, including some more complex language, mostly accurately

> To achieve grade 5 candidates will be able to: write clearly for different purposes, expressing ideas and opinions and manipulating vocabulary and grammar with reasonable accuracy

---

[30] **A. Grevatt & M. Evans** (2010). *Badger KS3 Science Year 7: Assessing Pupil Progress (APP) in Science: The Levelled-Assessment Approach.* Stevenage: Badger Publishing.

[31] **A. Chandler-Grevatt (Ed.)** P. Gardom Hulme, J. Locke & H. Reynolds (2014). *Activate 1. Oxford KS3 Science.* Oxford: Oxford University Press.

[32] **Ofqual** (2016). *Grade Descriptors for GCSE: MFL.* <https://www.gov.uk/government/publications/grade-descriptors-for-gcses-graded-9-to-1/grade-descriptors-for-gcses-graded-9-to-1-modern-foreign-languages> accessed 5 September 2017.

To achieve grade 2 candidates will be able to: convey meaning and express simple opinions in familiar contexts using a limited range of language with some accuracy.

As a teacher, you can draw out some key indicators from this information that can be used to inform objectives and outcomes. Now, these are particularly vague examples, and you may not always agree with what the government puts out there, but we have to deal with what we are given.

Step one is to look for the general objectives: the 'what'. For me, these seem to be to write for different purposes in the language to express ideas and opinions, and to justify ideas and opinions.

The learning outcomes ('how well' – again I look for the verbs), seem to be:

- grade 8: writes effectively... manipulates (more complex) vocabulary and grammar... mostly accurately

- grade 5: writes clearly... manipulates vocabulary and grammar... reasonable accuracy

- grade 2: conveys meaning... uses limited vocabulary... some accuracy.

Step two is to use the information in the curriculum content to predict what each outcome might look like, and apply more specific, meaningful objectives and outcomes. The teacher needs to decide (often with other teachers), on the difference between writing 'effectively' and 'clearly', and, regarding accuracy, on the meaning of 'some', 'reasonable' and 'mostly'.

Step three is to apply these general principles to writing objectives for 'Writing' in MFL lessons.

 How to

To use grade descriptors for designing objectives:

1. Locate grade descriptors from the examination board or government guidance.

2. Identify *what* learners need to be able to do as the general objectives.

3. Work out *how well* the learners need to do at each objective by identifying qualitative verbs and comparing their meanings.

4. Apply the general principles to more specific examples when designing your lesson objectives and outcomes.

5. Trial them, reflect on how well learners respond, and refine as necessary.

Learning objectives are used to inform assessment in the lesson (practices 7–9)

Planning your lesson is essential if you are trying to foster a formative culture (section 2c), and particularly so if you are using learning objectives and outcomes to lead learning. There needs to be opportunity for learners to refer to the objectives regularly throughout the lesson to assess their progress against them.

There are a number of strategies that can aid this approach. A simple strategy is to plan three points in the lesson when the lesson objectives are revisited. For example, the start of the lesson develops a shared meaning, the middle of the lesson reflects on how far the objectives have been met and what still needs to be done, and the last part of the lesson can be spent reflecting on how well the objectives have been met. (This links to Schunk's 'observe, judge and react' opportunities shown in the research case study later in this section.)

Regular use of lesson objectives and moments for reflection through self-assessment or peer assessment (section 2h) allows learners to become used to checking their progress against the lesson objectives. Once they get into a routine, the teacher can encourage them to focus on the self-reflection, self-evaluation and self-regulation that we are aspiring to for our learners.

Checklists, learning ladders and rubrics (section 2f) can support this process, as the assessment criteria form the thread of the lesson, and hence the focus of a task, activity or learning episode, so the teacher and learners have a shared understanding of what they are learning and what success looks like. These can support the use of learning objectives throughout the lesson (practices 7 and 9).

Questions to help learners

Use the learning objectives as prompts:

- What have you learned so far? What do you need to do next?

- What can you do now that you couldn't at the beginning of the lesson?

- How much better are you at x than you were at the start of the lesson?

Perhaps list these as part of your questioning in your lesson plan (see section 2c).

Using learning objectives in plenaries

The last part of the lesson is essential for reflecting on learning (practice 8). Teachers need to plan time and stick to it for the plenary. The plenary can take many forms but it should:

- refer to the learning objectives

- address the learning objectives to reflect on how well each one has been met

- focus on what has been learned

- recognise next steps in learning.

In the UK, it is common for teachers to use the 'thumbs-up' method or 'traffic light' cards to check the progress of the whole class. The thumbs-up method can be used to indicate how well a learner has learned something. The learner holds out their thumbs upwards if they are confident, horizontally if they are unsure and facing down if they are not at all confident. The traffic light system uses cards coloured green, orange and red. Learners hold up the card that best reflects how well they feel they have met the objective. However, these methods have limitations: the teacher cannot actually assess how well the learners have learned each objective, and there is room for learners to be less than honest or accurate in their reflections.

Such methods can be far more effective if used to assess the actual learning. So, for example, the traffic light cards could represent three categories, with the teacher asking questions to see the whole-class response via a show of cards. In a food technology class, for example, the teacher could check knowledge and understanding of objectives relating to food groups: the red card indicating protein, orange for fat, and green for carbohydrate. The teacher could plan the questions to ask in the plenary to check knowledge and understanding: 'Which food group does bread belong to?' 'Which food group can cause heart disease if eaten in excess?' and so on.

There are many applications of this method in most subjects and it is a quick and effective way of checking knowledge and understanding, not just learner's perceived confidence. The teacher can use the information to inform the next lesson, depending on how well the class have done.

Goal setting and self-efficacy

This paper looks at several interacting factors, including the setting of goals (essentially, learning objectives), which influence learners' academic success. I have chosen this paper because, in considering the social aspects of learning,[33] it is relevant to several sections of this chapter. Although the study focuses on reading and writing, its ideas are being applied to learning in general.

Schunk, D.H. (2003). Self-efficacy for reading and writing: Influence of modelling, goal setting, and self-evaluation. *Reading & Writing Quarterly*, 19(2), 159–172.

This is a discussion paper without research questions per se, but which aimed to do the following:

- Discuss theory, research and applications relevant to one type of self-belief: self-efficacy

- Summarise research on reading and writing that highlights the important roles played by self-efficacy, modelling, goal setting, and self-evaluation.

The thrust of the study is based on learners' beliefs about their ability to learn something. This is called 'perceived self-efficacy', and is important in a learner's motivation to tackle a task in which they will learn. The underlying theory is that achievement is dependent on the interaction of a number of factors: learner behaviours, personal factors and environmental conditions.

A learner's personal beliefs influence their self-efficacy, which impacts on their motivation and their engagement with learning, and thus achievement. For me, this paper emphasises the role of the teacher in maximising a learner's self-efficacy. This is achieved through the values the teacher promotes and their reactions to a learner's response to a task.

Setting goals, such as learning objectives, is recognised as essential in the learning process. Schunk identifies the role of goals at the three stages of learning. At the start, the types of goals can be learning new knowledge and skills, completing the task or getting desired grades; during the task or tasks learners 'observe, judge and react' to their progress against the goals; and at the end they evaluate their progress against the goals. If a learner sees a difference between their performance and the goal, this can increase effort.

---

[33] The paper draws on Albert Bandura's social cognitive theory: **A. Bandura** (1986). *Social Foundations of Thought and Action*. Englewood Cliffs, NJ: PrenticeHall.

Teachers have an important role in constructing learning goals that are specific, timely, and appropriately difficult. The more specific they are, the higher the self-efficacy potential. The sooner the goal can be achieved, the greater the motivation, particularly for younger learners. Moderately difficult tasks raise challenge, motivation, and thus self-efficacy.

Teachers can help learners to perceive how well they have done when evaluating their progress against a goal. Receiving quality 'goal progress feedback' helps them understand their progress, raising their motivation and self-efficacy.

The vocabulary that teachers use to achieve this is essential and something I will highlight in the practices described throughout Chapter 2. What you say and how you say it can make a difference.

Schunk concludes (p. 170):

Regardless of the content area, it is imperative that teachers develop and sustain their students' self-efficacy for learning. Research shows that self-efficacy and achievement can be enhanced through instructional methods that incorporate modelled strategies, progress feedback, goal setting, and self-evaluations of progress. *To the extent that these and other efficacy-enhancing methods are employed in classrooms, teachers will foster academic achievement and motivation for continued learning among all learners.*

Learners contribute to designing lesson objectives (practice 10)

Involving learners in the development of objectives for a learning episode is the epitome of allowing learners to be at the centre of learning and assessment. An example case study is described in section 2d, where primary school learners produce ideas about what they want to find out about ancient Egyptians.

In secondary school, this approach can be used to engage and motivate learners. Older learners can be apathetic, so a way to involve them is to ask them for questions that they want to answer. This gives them some ownership over the questions and the learning. Despite feeling constrained by examination requirements, teachers can still allow at least one or two objectives to be contributed in classes of older learners.

How to

To develop meaningful objectives:

- Use learning objectives to plan the teaching, learning and assessment.
- Use language that is specific and 'measurable' for learning objectives.
- Use strategies to engage the learners with the learning objectives.
- Create conditions that support learner motivation to achieve the objectives and outcomes.
- Provide opportunities within the lesson for learners to reflect on their progress against the objectives.
- Plan a plenary session that allows learners to reflect on their progress against the objectives and decide next steps in learning.

2f) Developing meaningful success criteria and rubrics

Creating a formative classroom culture through success criteria and rubrics

Success criteria and rubrics have similar features; they set out not only what will be assessed, but also describe the relative quality of the outcomes.

Both these approaches offer opportunities for formative assessment, through creating a shared meaning of expectations and opportunities for self-regulation. They are presented and used in a variety of ways, and can be adapted to suit the needs of all learners. This section looks at how these strategies can be implemented in a range of classroom cultures, with the aim of increasing formative practices and opportunities.

Towards a formative culture when using success criteria or rubrics

There are various types of success criteria and rubrics, three of which I will explore in this section. Sometimes **checklists** ('tick lists') can act as success criteria, often summarising the learning outcomes of several lessons (figure 2f1). A method I became fond of is the **learning ladder**, which communicates the success criteria through descriptors at each 'level' of learning (figure 2f2). Learning ladders are often more accessible to the younger end of high school learners, while **rubrics** – often more complex – are often used with

Defining success criteria and rubrics

Success criteria have the following features:

- often are related to an activity that is carried out in a lesson
- provide guidance for expected outcomes, usually a short description of low, mid and high attainment
- can be used to inform progress and judge outcomes of a lesson.

Rubrics have the following features:[34]

- clarify learning goals
- communicate learning goals
- are designed to address learning goals
- guide suitable feedback
- help judge the final product.

older learners. However, both learning ladders and rubrics can be made as simple or as complex as required.

As I explained in section 2a, it's not what you do, but the way that you do it. All these activities can be used in a summative way, but are most effective in improving learning and attainment if a formative approach is used. They become formative when the teacher and learners construct a shared meaning of the success criteria or rubric and can apply that through attempting a task, reflecting on a task and improving the task This way, learners are guided through the process of becoming confident, self-reflective and self-regulated learners.

There are key researchers in the area of using rubrics in formative assessment; of particular interest to me are Heidi Andrade in the US[35,36] and Ernesto Panadero in Spain.[37] In this section I will be drawing on research predominately by these researchers. I use a literature review by Panadero as the research case study.

My experience of writing learning ladders over a number of years to meet the changing needs of the national curriculum for England has shown me that

[34] **D.D. Stevens & A.J. Levi** (2012). *Introduction to Rubrics: An Assessment Tool to Save Grading Time, Convey Effective Feedback, and Promote Student Learning.* Sterling VA: Stylus.

[35] **H.G. Andrade** (2000). Using rubrics to promote thinking and learning. *Educational Leadership.* 57(5), 13–19.

[36] **H.L. Andrade, Y. Du & K. Mycek** (2010). Rubric-referenced self-assessment and middle school students' writing. *Assessment in Education: Principles, Policy & Practice*, 17(2), 199–214.

[37] **E. Panadero & M. Romero** (2014). To rubric or not to rubric? The effects of self-assessment on self-regulation, performance and self-efficacy. *Assessment in Education: Principles, Policy & Practice*, 21(2), 133–148.

Literacy checklist

Make sure you have:

- ☐ written with the **audience** in mind
- ☐ started each **sentence** with a **capital letter**
- ☐ written **correct sentences** (e.g. with full stops at the end, correct use of commas)
- ☐ organised your sentences into **paragraphs**
- ☐ checked your **spelling** of simple words and science key words
- ☐ used **apostrophes** to show contraction and possession.

Figure 2f1: An example of a checklist of success criteria

there are some aspects that work well and others less so. Each of the main ways of sharing success criteria – checklist, learning ladder and rubric[38] – has its distinctive value in supporting a formative classroom culture.

Checklist characteristics

Checklists (figure 2f1) are tick lists to record how far criteria have been met. They are sometimes presented as 'can-do' lists. These are a quick and easy way for learners to start to self-regulate, check on progress and self-correct.

Learning ladder characteristics

Learning ladders (figure 2f2) are lists of success criteria grouped into different levels of demand. These have an additional dimension over checklists, as they differentiate between levels of success. These can help to communicate not only what needs to be done, but how well it should be done.

 Also see

This section builds on section 2c) Planning meaningful assessment. It relates directly to section 2e) Developing meaningful objectives.

The section will also help with:

- 2g) Giving meaningful and effective feedback
- 2h) Meaningful self- and peer assessment

---

[38] **S.M. Brookhart** (2013). *How to Create and Use Rubrics for Formative Assessment and Grading*. Alexandria VA: ASCD.

Task

Draw a poster that explains why an ice cube melts when left out of the freezer.

Task sheet (levels 3–5)

How does an ice cube melt?

Some students were watching an ice cube in a beaker as it slowly melted. They were wondering why it melts.

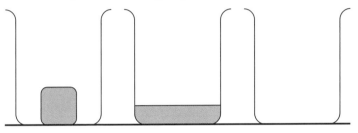

Key words

gas, liquid, solid

float, flow, hard, heavy, light, pouring, runny, steam, wet

compressible, shape, size, volume

boiling, evaporating, freezing, melting, solidification

fixed, moving randomly, particles, states of matter, vibrating

Level ladder

What is your target level? Use the level ladder to help you reach it:

To get level	You might have:
3	• Drawn a melting ice cube. • Stated what solids, liquids and gases are like.
4	• Used most key words correctly. • Described what solids, liquids and gases are like. • Used the correct words for each state. • Named and described the changes between each state.
5	• Drawn a simple particle diagram for each state. • Described some differences between the particle arrangement of each state. • Described the particle movements.

Figure 2f2: An example of a learning ladder, from *Badger Key Stage 3 Science: Level-Assessed Tasks – for Year 7,* Badger Publishing Ltd. Adapted by permission of Badger Publishing Ltd.

Rubric characteristics

Rubrics (table 2f1) are often in the form of a matrix that divides a task or assessment into domains to be assessed (see first column), and then provides the range of outcomes possible.

Where success criteria and rubrics fit in

Figure 2f3 illustrates where in the classroom assessment model the use

Table 2f1: Example of a rubric

Writing a paragraph	Good	Better	Best
Structure	At least three sentences	First sentence introduces the topic	First sentence introduces the topic. Last sentence states a conclusion or summary
Sentences	Full sentences are used	Sentences have some variation	Variation in sentence structure used
Punctuation	All sentences start with a capital letter and end with a full stop	Some sentences may contain commas	A range of punctuation used correctly
Connectives	No connectives used	Some connectives used	Varied connectives used appropriately
Spelling	Several spelling errors	A few spelling errors	All spellings checked and corrected

of success criteria and rubrics fits. Both will be informed by curriculum statements and inform the learning activities of the lesson. Success criteria and rubrics can form the underlying structure of the three pillars of objectives, outcomes and targets, supporting teaching and learning using a common understanding of expectations.

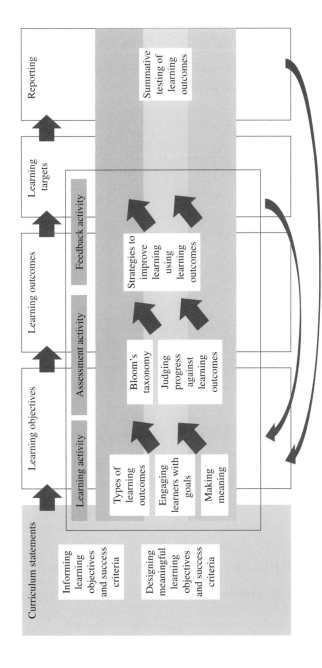

Figure 2f3: Where success criteria and rubrics fit in the classroom assessment model

Phases towards meaningful success criteria and rubrics

Figure 2f4 represents the suggested phases towards making success criteria and rubrics effective when fostering a formative assessment culture. Each phase is linked to the practices I will discuss in the rest of this section.

To help you establish which phase you are in and how to develop your practice, use the practice analyser (table 2f2).

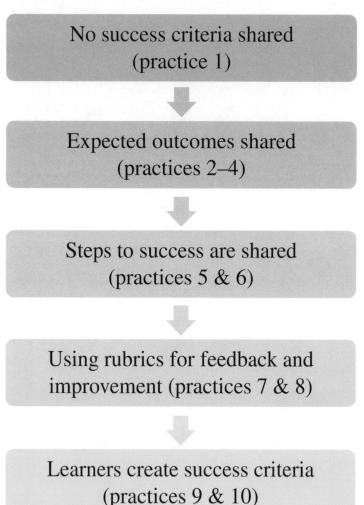

Figure 2f4: Towards developing meaningful criteria and rubrics

Using rubrics for formative assessment

 **Evidence**

I have chosen an up-to-date research literature review as the focus for this research case study. The review was carried out by two researchers, working in Spain and Sweden respectively. They searched extensively for research on the formative use of rubrics, finding and analysing 21 peer reviewed documents published 2001–2011. Here I summarise the findings relevant to this section.

Panadero, E. & Jonsson, A. (2013). The use of scoring rubrics for formative assessment purposes revisited: A review. *Educational Research Review*, 9, 129–144.

Research questions

- In what ways can the formative use of rubrics mediate improved student performance?

- Which factors may moderate the effects of using rubrics formatively?

Findings

Formative use of rubrics may improve student performance as follows:

- *Increased transparency*: It improves learners' performance by letting them know what is expected.

- *Reducing anxiety*: Because learners know what is expected of them and how they will be graded, they will be less anxious, and therefore perform better.

- *Aids the feedback process*: Teachers find rubrics useful for providing feedback; learners report they use rubrics to understand feedback.

- *Improves student self-efficacy*: Learners with high levels of self-efficacy tend to perform better than those with lower levels; however, rubrics may increase learners' self-efficacy.

- *Supports student self-regulation*: Rubrics can support self-assessment and self-regulation because the task is transparent; for example, students use the rubric to check they have covered everything.

Factors which affect the formative use of rubrics

- *Combining rubrics with meta-cognitive activities*: Most research uses rubrics along with other interventions, so it is not always clear to what extent the rubric on its own improves performance.

- *Educational level and length of interventions*: Rubrics are effective in higher education contexts, but in schools it takes longer to see the benefits. Younger learners need time to learn to work with a rubric.

- *Gender*: Although further research is needed, the findings suggest that girls perform better than boys when using a rubric.

Other factors that may moderate the effectiveness of rubrics include *accessibility of language*, *socio-economic factors*, and the *context of other tests*.

The research suggests that the *topic* does not change the effect of using a rubric. Rubrics can be used to assess a range of topics and performances (such as project design, critical thinking, landscape analysis…).

What still needs to be researched

The purpose of academic literature review is to ascertain what we currently know and what other research is required. Of relevance here is the need identified for further research on:

- the effect of different designs of rubric (such as holistic or analytical, few levels versus several levels, task-specific versus generic)

- personal differences in the use of rubrics

- the role of rubrics in self-regulation

- the effects of gender and rubric use.

Practice analyser: Developing meaningful success criteria and rubrics

Go through the questionnaire (table 2f2) and, for each statement, tick the box that best illustrates your use of that practice.

To analyse your results, first identify the best-fit description for your practices. For example, are your responses mostly in the 'rarely' or 'never' categories? If so, you are likely to be in the 'no success criteria shared' phase, so you would benefit from reading and applying practices 1–4. But first, here is some more information on practices and potential next steps.

Table 2f2: Practice analyser: Towards meaningful success criteria and rubrics

	Practice	Regularly	Often	Sometimes	Rarely	Never
1	No success criteria are shared with learners.					
2	Success criteria are shared at task level.					
3	Success criteria are shared at learning level.					
4	I share ready-made rubrics with my learners.					
5	I develop my own rubrics for my learners.					
6	I actively engage my learners with using rubrics.					
7	I plan lessons using rubrics to assess learning.					
8	I plan lessons using rubrics to improve learning.					
9	Learners create own success criteria.					

Analysing your practice and deciding your next steps

Having established the practices you use, decide which practice you would like to develop. Note that the practices at the top of the list are more likely to happen within a classroom with a summative culture, and they get progressively more likely to happen in a formative one. Think about your school assessment culture and your own assessment beliefs and values so that you can make an achievable next step to improve your classroom assessment practice.

Mostly 'rarely'/'never'

If you do not share the intended success criteria with your learners, then there are some approaches you can try (practices 1–4). These will help your learners understand what they are aiming for – what success looks like. This exposes the gap between where learners are and where they need to be, enabling you and your learners to develop a more formative culture.

Mostly 'sometimes'

If you sometimes do most of these practices, choose one or two you would like to develop. Carefully think about your school and classroom culture and consider which practices might benefit you in developing a more formative culture and improve teaching, learning and assessment in your lessons. You may want to focus on improving just one practice, such as sharing success criteria (choose from practices 2–4) or sharing steps to success (choose from practices 5–7).

Mostly 'regularly'/'often'

In the case of mostly 'regularly' or 'often' answers; if you have identified a practice that is 'sometimes', perhaps this is the one you may wish to develop, especially if it is lower down the table. If you are already using each of these practices, you may want to evaluate how effectively you are using them. Reading one of the sections may help you analyse your implementation and give you new ideas to try and develop, such as practice 9, where learners create their own success criteria.

If you have fully established these practices, then look at another section of Chapter 2 to see what you might like to improve.

 Reflection

Think about how you could use meaningful success criteria and rubrics. Decide on *one* area of practice that would help improve your classroom assessment. Consider the constraints you have from your school culture and your own aspirations for a more formative classroom. Think what is achievable and what is likely to have the most success and impact on teaching, learning and assessment.

- Read the pages that relate to that practice or set of practices.
- Choose one class to trial the activities with.
- Reflect on how your practice has changed and the impact on teaching, learning and assessment.

No expected outcomes shared with learners (practice 1)

Think about why you don't share success criteria and about the opportunities there might be if you did. As the research case study shows from the literature review, rubrics can aid formative assessment and learners' learning by providing a list of: things to be done (task); things to learn (process); and ways to learn (self-regulation).

If you work in a summative culture, you may first want to experiment with practice 2, where you share expected outcomes at the task level. This will familiarise learners with the idea that there are different outcomes for the same task. However, if you and your learners are ready to move straight to a focus on learning knowledge, understanding or skills, then have a look at practice 3 and try some of the approaches that exemplify expectations of learning.

Success criteria shared at task level (practice 2)

In addition to giving students learning objectives, as discussed in section 2e, you can provide expected outcomes framed as success criteria. The advantages of this are that the learners know the expectation – what success in the lesson looks like. This can be done at the start of the lesson simply by adding three headings under the learning objective and a description of the outcome. The following two examples share with learners an expectation of what they should achieve in the lesson.

Two ways of framing success criteria

1 **Must, should, could**

Objective: *To round up positive numbers to the nearest 10, 100 and 1000*

Learners must: *Complete exercises 1–10 on pages 92–93*

Learners should: *Complete the worksheet 'Rounding up'*

Learners could: *Try the worksheet 'Rounding up puzzlers'.*

2 **All, most, some**

Objective: *To round up positive numbers to the nearest 10, 100 and 1000*

All learners will: *Round up numbers to the nearest 10 or 100*

Most learners will: *Round up numbers to the nearest 10, 100 or 1000*

Some learners will: *Justify how you round up numbers to the nearest 10, 100 or 1000.*

Now it's all very well making the outcomes explicit at the start of the lesson, but to make the process formative, encouraging learners to become more self-reflective and self-regulating, it is important to provide opportunities for learners to reflect on what they have done and make improvements. In order to do this, teachers and learners must have a shared understanding of the success criteria.

In this practice, plan to have at least ten minutes for learners to reflect on what they have achieved in the lesson (see section 2c). Reflection can be done individually, or in pairs, (discussing their achievements with the learner next to them). If done at one or two points in the lesson, not only at the end, it serves to keep learners on task, focused and achieving the best they can in the lesson.

Although this practice does help learners know what is expected, it does not share with them the quality of learning that is required. Practice 3 describes how this can be achieved, by using and sharing more qualitative descriptors of success criteria.

Success criteria shared at learning level (practice 3)

This practice focuses on the *quality* of learning in the lesson, with communication of the depth of learning expected. In most situations, this is a relative scale of improvement; however, it can be used to indicate if a benchmark has been met. The latter works well in mastery-based assessment systems. The ways of sharing the quality of an outcome take many forms, from the mundane to the creative. Heather, a primary school teacher, shared this one with me that she uses for a literacy lesson in which learners have to write a list of instructions (table 2f3). A craze within schools in England is to use a 'chilli rating'. Heather uses the terms 'mild', 'spicy' and 'hot' alongside a visual cue of one, two or three chillies. The 'hotter' the task, the more challenging it is.

Table 2f3: Example of success criteria

Mild	Spicy	Hot
Capital letters	Time adverbials	Compound sentences to add detail
Full stops	Adjectives and adverbs when needed	
Imperative (bossy) verbs		

Here are a few more examples of labels for success criteria that I have seen used in classrooms:

a all aboard, getting there, reaching for the stars!

b good, better, best

c poor, good, excellent

d establishing, confident, advanced

e working towards, working at, exceeding.

All these labels have their strengths and limitations. Examples A and B are common in primary schools. My view is that, although it is fun, example A is not really communicating the depth of learning, just the tasks carried out (as described in practices 1 and 2). Example B does communicate clearly the relative quality of each outcome; the language is positive and encouraging. It assumes that everyone will achieve at least a good standard and there are two steps to be the best. Example C is a traditional approach to communicating how well a learner has done; these terms are often used when feeding back. However, the values do need to be assigned to the work, rather than the learner themselves. 'Poor' is a negative word and not helpful in motivating a learner to do better. More recently in the UK, where mastery-style approaches have started to be used in assessment, success criteria based on a benchmark can communicate how well a learner is doing. In example D, the word 'establishing' recognises that work has started but has not yet reached the benchmark: it is work in progress. 'Confident' suggests the benchmark has been reached, and 'advanced' that the learner has gone beyond it. Example E does something similar to D, but is more literal. Again, the language is encouraging rather than draconian. The following classroom case study shows Heather, a primary school teacher, using example E labels when teaching about the Great Fire of London.

The Great Fire of London 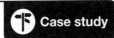 Case study

Heather uses three learning objectives, presented as 'I can' statements:

- I can say where the Great Fire of London started.

- I can state when the Great Fire of London took place.

- I can place the events on a time line showing periods in the history of England.

She then communicates the expected outcomes or success criteria at three levels of expectation, as shown in the following diagram.

Working towards	Working at	Exceeding
Cut out and stick pictures in the correct places on the timeline.	Write which events happened for each corresponding date on the timeline.	Order and write the dates and events of topics we have covered on a blank timeline.

This example is particularly relevant to practices 2 and 3. The advantage of the learning objectives and success criteria used here is that the learners will know exactly what should be done.

The success criteria focus on what the learners should do rather than what they should learn. However, they do increase in skill demand. The 'working towards' criteria are a supported activity, a 'cut and stick', that reduces the task to just placing the pictures on a time line. The benchmark expectation is that all learners should be able to write the events in the correct places on the timeline, hopefully learning the key points required by the objectives. For learners to work beyond the expectation requires much more independence; drawing and labelling their own timeline.

These criteria could be used to aid formative assessment during and at the end of the lesson. The learning objectives are clearly assessable and could be ascertained through questioning at the end of the lesson. Learners can judge how successful they have been, based on how they have tackled the activity.

For the success criteria to be improved, I would suggest linking the activities to the learning required. Perhaps the learning objectives could be:

- Describe the main events of the Great Fire of London (knowledge and understanding).

- Create a timeline to show major historical events (skill).

The success criteria could be revised as shown in the following diagram.

Working towards	Working at	Exceeding
I can state when and where the fire started. I can place events in the correct order along a timeline.	I can describe the main dates and events of the Great Fire of London. I can write events on the correct places on a timeline.	I can describe in detail the events of the Great Fire of London. I can design a timeline of the main events.

Notice the links between the knowledge, understanding and skills communicated in the objectives and the wording of the success criteria: I have increased the demand of the learning objectives and adapted the language in the success criteria accordingly.

Sharing ready-made rubrics with my learners (practice 4)

In some countries, rubrics are produced by the government's education department (e.g. *Assessing Pupil Progress* in England in 2005[39]), by local school authorities or groups of schools (e.g. criteria-based assessment in NIS

---

[39] **Department for Education** (2005). *Assessing Pupil Progress*. London: Crown Publishing. <http://webarchive.nationalarchives.gov.uk/20110202142353/ http://nationalstrategies.standards.dcsf.gov.uk/primary/assessment/ assessingpupilsprogressapp> accessed 5 September 2017.

schools in Kazakhstan[40]), or by publishers (in North America, for example). A quick online search of 'rubric + stage + subject' will reveal many rubrics produced by teachers from around the world.

A good starting point may be to look at the variety of rubrics available and get ideas for the type of rubric you may want to use. Ready-made rubrics are useful in many ways, as the deeper thinking has already been done for you and they are often ready to use. Just print copies of them and give them to your learners. However, the disadvantages are that the rubric may not be specific enough for your class or lesson, the language used may not be appropriate or accessible for your class, and it may be designed to assess different areas from those you are interested in, or required to assess. There are a number of features to consider.

What makes a suitable rubric?

To have a successful experience of using a rubric for the first time, it is important that you use a rubric that is appropriate for your situation. I originally called this section 'what makes a *good* rubric', and although there are some *desirable* features in a rubric (amongst the plethora of available rubrics, quality varies), what is more important is that the rubric is suitable for your learners.

Selecting a suitable rubric

Some features are *essential* when selecting a rubric:

- Does it match your learning objectives?

- Is the language accessible to your learners?

- Are you able to use it to share meaning of the success criteria with the learners?

- Is there clear increase in demand for each descriptor for each domain?

Other features are *desirable*:

- Do the attainment labels use positive language?

- Do the descriptors use qualitative indicators such as Bloom's verbs (see section 2c)?

- Does it fit into the bigger picture of assessment in your lessons?

---

[40]**Nazerbayez International School** <http://nis.edu.kz/en/programs/criter-eval/> accessed 5 September 2017.

Once you have tried and tested a few rubrics, you may wish to try developing your own, which I discuss in practice 5.

Developing your own rubrics (practice 5)

It takes practice and lots of trial and error to write an effective and meaningful rubric. There are multiple challenges – creating them is often like a problem-solving activity in itself. I relish the challenge and really enjoy the process, as well as the satisfaction of writing a rubric which learners can use effectively.

The advantages for teachers in creating their own rubrics include:

- developing a clear understanding of the assessment and the task being set
- engaging with assessment criteria
- considering the range of possible outcomes
- identifying key steps in learning for a learner to be successful
- establishing a bigger picture of assessment and progress.

In this section, I will describe the steps I take when writing a rubric and illustrate this with some examples from England and Kazakhstan. In the first instance, we need to consider the key features of a rubric. There are two dimensions to any rubric: the assessed domains and the descriptors:

- *Domains* are the areas that will be assessed (often knowledge, understanding, skills, application, and communication).
- *Descriptors* are used to communicate the range of quality of the assignment. These can be based on grading information or a recognised educational progression scale.

The key aspects to keep in mind when writing any rubric include:

- Which domains will be assessed?
- What are the descriptors based upon (Bloom's, examination grade criteria, etc.)?
- What are the learning objectives?
- What are the key instructions for the task?

Presenting success criteria

Learning ladders present success criteria in a one-dimensional way, whereas a rubric presents the success criteria in a two-dimensional matrix.

Table 2f4: A generic learning ladder

Grade	Descriptor (for each domain)
Grade 1	Domain A descriptor for grade 1 Domain B descriptor for grade 1 Domain C descriptor for grade 1 Domain D descriptor for grade 1
Grade 2	Domain A descriptor for grade 2 Domain B descriptor for grade 2 Domain C descriptor for grade 2 Domain D descriptor for grade 2
Grade 3	Domain A descriptor for grade 3 Domain B descriptor for grade 3 Domain C descriptor for grade 3 Domain D descriptor for grade 3

The learning ladder presents the descriptors for each 'grade', with each domain exemplified by the descriptor (table 2f4). I used this method with my published level ladders,[41] where each level had the five domains covered. These were usually descriptors for:

- a generic statement about the task (for example, 'produce an informative leaflet that compares different types of house insulation')

- the knowledge and understanding (to be covered)

- the skills (the scientific skills required)

- the numeracy (how numbers, units and statistics are used)

- the literacy (use of key words and presentation).

Learning ladders are often easy for learners to access when they are completing a piece of work and aiming for a particular level of attainment.

The learning matrix is often slightly more detailed, but uses exactly the same types of information as the learning ladder; it is just presented differently. It fragments the descriptors required for each grade, and some learners find it easier to assess work using this format. Table 2f5 shows how a learning matrix rubric uses descriptors for each domain and grade combination.

---

[41] **A. Grevatt & M. Evans** (2010). *Badger KS3 Science Year 7: Assessing Pupil Progress (APP) in Science: The Levelled-Assessment Approach.* Stevenage: Badger Publishing.

Table 2f5: A generic learning matrix

	Grade 1	Grade 2	Grade 3
Domain A	Descriptor for domain A at grade 1.	Descriptor for domain A at grade 2.	Descriptor for domain A at grade 3.
Domain B	Descriptor for domain B at grade 1.	Descriptor for domain B at grade 2.	Descriptor for domain B at grade 3.
Domain C	Descriptor for domain C at grade 1.	Descriptor for domain C at grade 2.	Descriptor for domain C at grade 3.
Domain D	Descriptor for domain D at grade 1.	Descriptor for domain D at grade 2.	Descriptor for domain D at grade 3.

Defining the purpose of the rubric

Rubrics can be used to describe learning outcomes for a number of purposes. These purposes can be descriptors of learning outcomes for: an academic year; an academic term; a specific topic; a specific concept or skill; a specific activity or assignment.

Sometimes teachers develop and use generic rubrics that can be used whenever a particular activity is carried out. For example, in English lessons there could be a rubric for analysing a poem or for writing a discursive essay; in science there could be a rubric for presenting data in graphs or evaluating experiments; and in a foreign language class, a rubric for using different tenses or for checking written work. The advantage of these is that they can be reused whenever the learner encounters the skill or activity, ensuring that they reflect on their past performance and how they may improve in the new situation.

Often rubrics are specific for a class (year group or school grade) and specific activity. They work best when they bring together the learning from a series of lessons and apply the new skills to the new task. This is the method I used for all level ladders: they were designed to be used towards the end of a topic to bring together knowledge, understanding and skills, assess current understanding, and intervene to make improvements before an end-of-unit test.

Selecting domains

Domains are what is going to be assessed, and the number of domains can vary depending on the complexity and length of the activity to be assessed. Common areas include: knowledge and understanding; skills; application of knowledge, understanding and skills; communication. However, rubrics can be used to assess other domains, for example: ability to work in a group; ability to work independently; ability to search for, select and use secondary resources; ability to work as part of a sports team; critical thinking; self- or peer assessment. These are often seen as 'soft skills', but are often important domains to consider when improving social, emotional and learning skills. So don't forget that these can be considered, particularly drawing on the affective domain of Bloom's taxonomy (see section 2c).

When deciding on domains, it is often helpful to define them. An early incarnation of the criteria-based assessment initiative in Kazakhstan NIS schools used the following domains across most subjects: knowledge and understanding; skills; application; and communication (table 2f6). The description helps define the purpose of the domain, focus on what is to be assessed, and relate it to the overall curriculum aims and objectives.

Table 2f6: An example of domains for criteria-based assessment

	Domain	Brief description
A	Knowledge and understanding	In general terms, what students should know and understand about the subject at this particular school grade.
B	Skills	In general terms, what students should be able to do for this subject at this particular school grade. This can be subject-specific: for biology, chemistry or physics it will be practical and investigative skills; for geography it may be research skills and map reading; for physical training it will be coordination, team sports, etc.
C	Application	In general terms, the contexts in which students should be able to apply knowledge, understanding and skills at this particular school grade. This can include applying the subject to everyday situations or its relevance in society. It can include social, ethical, economic, environmental or technological applications.
D	Communication	In general terms, how students should be able to communicate this subject at this particular school grade. This can include using conventions specific to the subject, producing charts or graphs, using specific notation, and speaking, reading, listening and written skills.

Selecting grading

The grading can be based on generic criteria or specific curricula guidance (school, national or examination board). Bloom's taxonomy can be used as a generic source of grading or it can be used in combination with curricula guidance. I will discuss grades and grading in section 2i, but, as discussed in practice 3, the grades can use a variety of labels to communicate the performance, attainment or achievement.

If we take the simple example of the 'assignment' of making a cup of English breakfast tea, we can imagine the grades as 'establishing', 'confident', and 'advanced' (see table 2f7). This example is relevant when writing descriptors, discussed next.

Writing descriptors

The most common mistake in writing descriptors is giving away the answer. The descriptors must communicate clearly what the learner must achieve, and how well it should be achieved, but give nothing away about how to achieve it.

Table 2f7: An exemplar learning ladder for making a cup of tea

Learning objective: To make a cup of English breakfast tea Domain A General outcome: a cup of tea is made and served Domain B Skill: the equipment and ingredients are used effectively Domain C Safety: appropriate safety precautions are taken Domain D Presentation: The presentation of the cup of tea	
Grade	**Descriptors (for each domain)**
Grade 1: **Establishing**	You make and serve a cup of tea to the appropriate strength *or* temperature range. Select *some* appropriate equipment and use it, *with some help*, to make the cup of tea. Make the cup of tea safely, considering all safety precautions and without any major spillages. Present the cup of tea.
Grade 2: **Confident**	You make and serve a cup of tea to the appropriate strength and temperature range. Select appropriate equipment and use it effectively to make the cup of tea. Make the cup of tea safely, considering all safety precautions and without any major spillages. Present the cup of tea, using a tray.
Grade 3: **Advanced**	You make and serve a cup of tea to the appropriate strength and temperature. Select appropriate equipment and use it effectively to make the cup of tea. Make the cup of tea safely, considering all safety precautions and without any spillages. Present the cup of tea, using a tray, with saucer, spoon and milk.

Developing the learning ladders

This is my quick guide to writing a successful learning ladder or rubric matrix:

- Decide on the terminology you will use to communicate the different levels of quality – such as grades 1–5, grades A–E, or qualitative terms such as 'good, better, best'.

- Decide on the domains that will be assessed, such as knowledge and understanding, skills, communication.

- Decide on the task and make sure it meets the learning objectives and success criteria.

- Carefully write descriptors that best describe the success criteria for each domain at each quality:

  - Start with a summarising sentence that gives the gist of the task at that quality (e.g. for domain D, 'Appropriate safety precautions are taken').

  - State what the learner should demonstrate (what they know, understand or can do) in relation to the domain.

  - Statements in each phase should relate directly to the task instructions.

  - Statements in each phase should be of a higher demand than in the previous phase.

  - Do not reveal the answer in the statements.

Remember, this takes time to get right. Don't be afraid to have a go, trial it, and reflect on it. Refine the language, descriptors and structure each time you trial it with a class.

Actively engaging learners with using rubrics (practice 6)

Practices 4 and 5 have discussed the key features of rubrics that can make them an effective teaching tool. However, even with all these features in place, the classroom culture has to have values that promote learning and self-regulation from learners.

As with all new activities, learners will need time to get accustomed to using a rubric. The teacher must actively introduce and engage learners with the rubric. Teachers and learners can learn how to use the rubric together, but the teacher must take the lead.

For example, the first time a rubric is used, the teacher must take time to introduce the activity, perhaps using the following ideas:

- Explain to the class the purpose of the activity.

- Communicate what you are looking for.

- Exemplify how the rubric can support the learner doing the task by talking through part of the rubric.

- Provide time for learners to read the rubric, then discuss it and ask questions.

Once rubrics have become an established part of the lesson, the teacher still needs to actively engage the learners with the rubric, so you could:

- plan the lesson so that the stages of rubric use are identified and supported (see practices 7 and 8)

- give time for learners to read the rubric and ask questions

- encourage learners to decide what they are aiming to achieve

- differentiate the rubric for those that require support with reading.

Plan lessons using rubrics to assess and improve learning (practices 7 and 8)

Using a rubric to assess learning (practice 7) can have both a summative and formative function. My experience of learning ladders was that teachers tended to use them for a summative outcome rather than a formative process. Even when learning targets were identified, often no time was given to aid improvement.

There are three main ways of using a rubric to assess learning: as a tick list of 'done' statements; a best-fit approach; or scoring converted into a grade.

The tick-list approach is best described as ticking off the descriptors that have been achieved. No grade or score is assigned. After a task has been completed, the learner's work is considered against the descriptors and those that have been achieved are identified. A variant on this binary assessment of achieved/ not achieved is when descriptors are described as 'partially achieved'.

The best-fit model uses the 'tick' method, but makes a judgement of the 'best fit' to assign a estimate of the quality of the work. For example, if a rubric has three descriptors for each grade; if all three descriptors are met in grade 3 but only two of grade 2, the 'best fit' is usually grade 3. (Some systems would expect all the descriptors to be met to achieve a grade – in this case the learner's work would be graded as grade 2.) If a learner's work meets two of the descriptors of grade 3 and two of the descriptors in grade 2, a judgement has to be made.

If the matrix rubric is used, then a grade for each domain can be decided and, if a single score or grade is required, an average can be calculated from all the domains (see example in table 2f8).

Table 2f8: A generic learning matrix with grade average calculated

	Grade 1	Grade 2	Grade 3	Grade achieved
Domain A	Descriptor for domain A at grade 1	Descriptor for domain A at grade 2	Descriptor for domain A at grade 3	2
Domain B	Descriptor for domain B at grade 1	Descriptor for domain B at grade 2	Descriptor for Domain B at grade 3	3
Domain C	Descriptor for domain C at grade 1	Descriptor for domain C at grade 2	Descriptor for domain C at grade 3	2
Average grade				2.3

I was involved at the start of an interesting project with Kazakhstan in the development of criteria-based assessment (CBA) in schools. I remember one lively conversation with Kazakh colleagues when we met an impasse in how the CBA grid should be used to assess the learners. Working through interpreters hinders understanding at the best of times, and it took me a while to realise that I was focused on words but my colleagues were focused on numbers. The schools needed a grade for each learner and that was the crux. This is a powerful example of a summative culture at odds with formative values, and one of those moments of realisation in my career that stays with me.

When using rubrics to grade learners' work, decisions have to be made. They are qualitative, criteria-based devices that require judgement calls. Teachers need to decide if a learner is getting information about 'at my best I can achieve...', or 'on average I achieve...'. I am always a bit cautious about assigning numbers and quantitative interpretations to rubrics, as it detracts from their formative purpose in the classroom. Stopping at the point of assigning a mark, grade or number using a rubric limits their potential to develop learners and improve their learning.

Rubrics show their real strength when used formatively. It doesn't matter exactly what score has been achieved – it is more important to focus on those next steps. A brief reference to learning theory: Lev Vygotsky[42] developed the

---

[42] **L.S. Vygotsky** (1980). *Mind In Society: The Development of Higher Psychological Processes.* Harvard: Harvard University Press.

idea of the 'zone of proximal development' (ZPD), which is the space where learners can learn with a 'more knowledgeable other' – often the teacher. The great thing about rubrics is that they expose that ZPD; then a teacher or a peer can support learning within that space. The unticked descriptors are the ZPD. As a teacher, you can decide with the learner the next steps in their learning, consider ways of tackling that step, and provide assistance in achieving it. (Section 2g explores way to give meaningful feedback.) When using the rubric, the conversation about what the learner needs to do next and the opportunity to do it is far more valuable than counting scores or trying to assign a grade.

Learners create their own success criteria (practice 9)

There are some benefits for learners to be engaged with creating their own success criteria.[43] It helps them become self-regulating, analytical, and engaged with the topic and how it could be assessed. Formative assessment puts learners at the heart of the process, so once they have experienced how to use success criteria, using their experience to create them could be the next step.

As with all strategies, you will need to give learners guidance and support. Providing the learners with a structure they know (whether it is 'all, most, some' or the 'chilli scale') will scaffold their ideas. Here are examples I have seen or done myself, to help develop and contextualise this idea.

Designing posters or leaflets

There are many opportunities for learners to produce a poster or a leaflet about a specific topic and in a particular style, such as an advertisement, public information brochure, instructions, scientific investigation, or persuasive literature (e.g. a political or advocacy group).

In an English lesson, for example, the learners were tasked with producing a persuasive leaflet. In order to determine the success criteria, the learners were given a collection of leaflets that met those criteria. The teacher asked the learners to list the common features of the literature (hinting at the importance of the language, headers and rhetoric used). Once they had decided these features, the learners were asked to rank the leaflets in order of least persuasive to most persuasive, and to justify their decisions. The teacher then asked the learners to write down the key success criteria for a 'good', 'better'

---

[43]Rubrics are another matter. As you will have found if you have tried writing your own rubrics, they are difficult to construct. They need careful wording, require deep understanding of how we learn and rely on some expertise in progression within a subject. So it is not something that is worthwhile for learners to do. What would be the point? What would learners gain from it?

and 'best' leaflet. This activity took about twenty minutes, but engaged the learners fully in the key features of persuasive writing, and provided examples across a quality range. When the learners had to produce their own persuasive leaflets, they were able to apply what they had learned and assess the leaflet against their own criteria. This models very much what we have to do in our professional lives, where, with support, learners become self-regulating.

Expressive arts

In an A level (post-16) dance lesson, the learners were tasked with choreographing a short dance routine in the style of Bob Fosse (an American choreographer). The learners had been set a homework activity to watch three online videos of Fosse's choreography. They were told that they should note down its key characteristics. The teacher then asked the group to agree and write down the key characteristics of Fosse's choreography. Once this had been decided, the teacher played a piece of music that the learners were to use to create a routine in the style of Fosse. There were three groups, and they gave feedback on each other's routines using their criteria. In this case, the learners formed a common understanding of a style of choreography and used this as the basis for success criteria through which they developed and refined their routines.

Secondary school art lesson 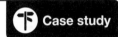 Case study

Rachel developed a rubric to use with a class using a wax-resist technique. I have chosen this example as a case study because it draws on many of the practices discussed in this section. It should give you the opportunity to consider how these ideas can be applied.

So, this art lesson was supported with some success criteria that Rachel created and used to support her planning and assessment in the lesson. Below are the learning objectives, structured as 'all, most, some'. The success criteria are then presented as a series of questions. These are shared with the learners, along with a 'student sheet' for use at the end of the lesson, where learners can self-assess. Note that on the student sheet Rachel has linked in grade criteria, shown in brackets.

Learning objectives

- *All*: will apply the wax-resist technique with some control and with some understanding of the success criteria
- *Most*: will apply the wax-resist technique with control and with a good understanding of the success criteria

---

147

- *Some*: will apply the wax-resist technique with control and flair and will apply all of the success criteria.

Success criteria for wax-resist studies

- Have you selected a relevant section of the double page? (Oil pastels are chunky and selection of highly detailed areas is therefore not appropriate.)
- Did you use the sharp edges of the pastels to create fine lines, where appropriate?
- Did you remember to use the colour wheel to inform your colour choices?
- Did you remember to use lighter colours for the pastel work and darker for the complementary (painted) colour?
- Did you remember to make the paint watery?
- Did you remember to use a 'lake' of yellow and a 'puddle' of red and blue poster paint?

Student sheet

Name: _____

Date:_____

All (KAD 3 Level 4 or above): will apply the wax-resist technique with some control and some understanding of the success criteria

Most (KAD 3 Level 5 or above): will apply the wax-resist technique with control and with a good understanding of the success criteria

Some (KAD 3 Level 6 or above): will apply the wax-resist technique with control and flair and will apply all of the success criteria

In today's lesson I worked at a level _____or above.

I know this because I have applied the wax-resist technique with _____control and I have applied_____of the success criteria to my work.

Case study commentary

I think it is useful to reflect on the school and classroom culture of this lesson. Think about the following questions:

- What are the assumptions of the teacher, given the learning objectives are 'all, most, some'?

- Which of the success criteria are based on the task, the process, or self-regulation?
- What are the advantages and disadvantages of including grades?
- What would the summative use of this resource look like?
- What would the formative use of this resource look like?

The language used in these success criteria is learner-friendly; I can see how Rachel has developed a shared meaning of the terms used. The 'did you remember to...?' phrases show that the success criteria are clearly based on prior learning. Rachel combines elements of tick-list and success criteria approaches.

The 'student sheet' allows learners to have reference to the success criteria throughout the lesson. I can imagine Rachel discussing their work using the success criteria. The structure of the student sheet gives opportunity for learners to reflect on their work, self-assess, and recognise the success criteria they have met.

The next steps for the students could be to identify the success criteria that have not been met. They could be given time to address next steps. I also wondered how the success criteria could be converted into a rubric, either a learning ladder or a matrix.

Summary of developing meaningful criteria and rubrics

Using the model for classroom assessment in figure 2g1, I have identified where and when success criteria and rubrics can be used effectively to be meaningful and formative. The planning stage is essential (see section 2c) so that the objectives, outcomes and feedback are linked concisely to the task or learning episode.

 How to

To develop meaningful success criteria and rubrics

- Consider what success looks like from your lesson objectives.
- Decide how you will share the success criteria of the lesson.
- Develop shared meaning of the success criteria.
- Choose how you will share expectations (checklist, learning ladder or rubric).
- Ensure that the success criteria support formative values.

2g) Giving meaningful and effective feedback

Creating a formative classroom culture through feedback

> At the end of the day people won't remember what you said or did; they will always remember how you made them feel.

This quote, widely attributed to Maya Angelou, North American writer and civil rights activist, is so valid for teachers. As teachers, we hope that learners will hang on to every word we say and respond positively to our feedback. We have to build relationships where learners feel safe, valued, and have a positive space to learn and make mistakes. What teachers give feedback on, and how they do so, has come under scrutiny by researchers, and we are still learning about the cultural, social and cognitive aspects of learning.

Classroom assessment feedback is the information provided to a learner to reduce the gap between the actual and desired learning outcome.[44] This feedback information can be provided by a teacher, a peer, a rubric, or even by digital devices.

One figure has transformed our understanding of the role of feedback in the assessment process: Professor John Hattie, a prolific education researcher working in Australia and New Zealand[45]. After conducting a huge set of meta-analyses (collating research papers to generate effect sizes for specific features of impact on learning), Hattie and his colleagues concluded that the most powerful impact on learners' attainment was effective feedback[46].

Hattie has produced a framework through which to understand when and how feedback is most effective. Hattie and Timperley's feedback model[47] summarises this with three feedback questions:

- Where am I going? (transparency of learning goals)

- How am I doing? (information on the current task performance)

---

[44]**D.R. Sadler** (1989). Formative assessment and the design of instructional systems. *Instructional Science*, 18, 119–144.

[45] **J. Hattie** (2008). *Visible Learning: A synthesis of over 800 meta-analyses relating to achievement*. Oxon: Routledge.

[46]**J. Hattie & H. Timperley** (2007). The power of feedback. *Review of Educational Research*, 77(1), pp. 81–112.

[47]**J. Hattie** (2012). *Visible Learning for Teachers: Maximizing impact on learning*. Oxon: Routledge.

- Where to next? (individual cues on how to reach desired task performance).

The last of these is becoming to be seen to be the most important. 'Where to next?' is about the time given to improvement.

The biggest shortcoming in the use of my level ladders in science was that teachers stopped at the 'how am I doing?' stage, relying on feedback that was task orientated. Learners were often given a grade and a target, but no action beyond that. The targets were not valued: they were not given attention at the time or revisited later in order for the learners to make improvements.

What meaningful feedback looks like

These approaches make the feedback meaningful. The feedback has value; it is part of a process, not an outcome. Research to date characterises meaningful feedback as task-related, specific, positive and timely.

Meaningful feedback uses success criteria directly related to the task and is specific about what the outcome should look like. Feedback should be framed positively, which I will explore later, and should be within a reasonable time of completing a task. Often immediate is best, but there is some evidence that, in some situations, a short delay is valuable.

Cultural aspects of giving feedback

There are cultural hurdles to overcome when teachers give feedback and learners respond to it. The traditional teacher–learner model is weighted in favour of the teacher. From the perspective of the learner, the teacher has the ability to pass or fail them, to influence how well they achieve, and to make their learning experience either positive or negative. In China, for example, your elders are perceived as wise, to be obeyed, and their judgements unquestioned.[48] These assumptions are deeply culturally embedded and take time to shift. Most learners, though certainly not all, have the desire to please their teacher. This is an important aspect for teachers to be aware of, as we have the power to change our expectations, slowly adjust what 'pleases' us, and thereby influence the culture of the classroom.

In basic terms, the traditional approach of ticks and crosses creates a binary effect. Learners want to get answers correct and things right because that's what they perceive the teacher wants. Learners who achieve this feel valued, motivated, and 'good at' the subject; the others end up feeling devalued, demotivated, and defined as 'not good' at that subject. A shift in focus from

---

[48]**D. Carless** (2012). *From Testing to Productive Student Learning: Implementing formative assessment in Confucian-heritage settings*. London: Routledge.

the outcome to the process of improvement – through making mistakes, identifying gaps in learning and taking action to fill them – means that every learner has an opportunity to make progress. Therefore, they will value the subject, feel more intrinsically motivated, and confident to learn.

Teachers have the power to create these classroom conditions. In this section, I will demonstrate a range of strategies that foster this formative, feedback-valuing and safe learning culture. This can be achieved through sharing expectations, reinforcing these expectations through actions, and valuing the learning and feedback process.

Sharing expectations helps focus teachers and learners on the task in hand and develop an understanding of what is required for a particular task. These expectations can be focused on different levels: task level; process level; self-regulation level; and self-level:

- *Task level*: focused on whether the task is completed correctly or not, what Hattie calls the 'information level'. This is the most common level of feedback given by teachers. I see this as 'how well do you need to complete the task?'

- *Process level*: focused on how the task could be tackled – what processes were used to learn, understand, achieve

- *Self-regulation level*: self-monitoring, directing, and regulating of actions

- *Self-level*: personal evaluations and effect (usually positive) on the learner.

It is also worth considering that when learners anticipate getting feedback, it actually motivates them and improves their achievement.[49]

 Also see

This section builds on 2c) Planning meaningful assessment.

It links directly to:

- 2e) Developing meaningful objectives
- 2f) Developing meaningful success criteria and rubrics

Its value will be enhanced by looking at:

- 2d) Questioning your questioning
- 2h) Meaningful self- and peer assessment

---

[49] **R. Pekrun, A. Cusack, K. Murayama, A.J. Elliot & K. Thomas** (2014). The power of anticipated feedback: Effects on students' achievement goals and achievement emotions. *Learning and Instruction*, 29, 115–124.

Digital feedback

The use of digital technology by teachers and learners varies dramatically from school to school and from country to country. In the UK, there are schools where every learner has a tablet computer and others where students have limited access to desktop computers housed in computer rooms that teachers must book for lessons. Some schools allow learners to use their mobile phones as a resource in lessons; other schools ban mobile phone use. The Kazakh schools I visited had computer rooms, but I did not see learners using mobile phones in school. The technology infrastructure was developing; teachers had laptops, but registers and reports were still done on paper. Although practice varies, digital technology is a huge opportunity for feedback.

Feedback through digital technology, be it via smartphones, tablets or laptops, has been shown to be highly effective in giving informative and individualised feedback.[50] Although such approaches are useful, teacher involvement is imperative to create the conditions that support, motivate, and mediate the use of digital activities. Learners can leave feeling demotivated from poor outcomes or unrealistically confident from good outcomes.

In this section, consider that feedback is part of the classroom assessment process. It is a multi-faceted process, but with a few checks, feedback can become meaningful to both learner and teacher.

Where giving feedback fits in

Feedback activities bridge between the learning outcomes (however they are communicated) and the learning targets, as illustrated in figure 2g1. Learning outcomes and targets could be from the same source. For example, a learning ladder has all the success criteria listed; those that have not been achieved become the targets.

Feedback to move learners from one level of demand to the next can take many forms. It can be verbal or written, be provided by the teacher, a peer, or the learner themselves, and it can be immediate or delayed. Finally, the extended feedback loop can inform the teacher of how to teach either the class they have or future classes, and the learners can have general feedback from a lesson or from a summative test.

---

[50] **A.M. Johnson, J. Reisslein & M. Reisslein** (2015). Transitional feedback schedules during computer-based problem-solving practice. *Computers & Education*, 81, 270–280.

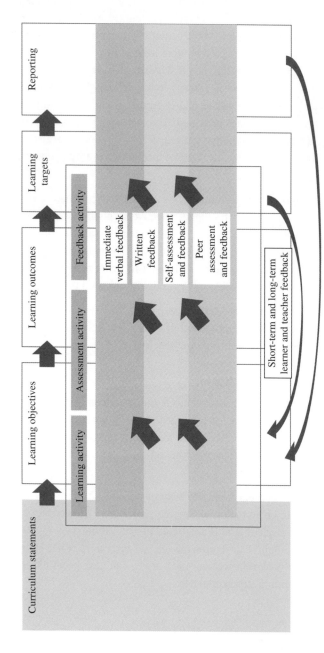

Figure 2g1: A model for classroom assessment: Where giving feedback fits in

Transparency of learning goals

This research case study illustrates how the effectiveness of rubrics can be improved through the teacher's use of specific feedback. I have chosen it because it uses an experimental design, thus building on many qualitative studies about the factors that affect response to feedback.

Wollenschläger, M., Hattie, J., Machts, N., Möller, J. & Harms, U. (2016). What makes rubrics effective in teacher-feedback? Transparency of learning goals is not enough. *Contemporary Educational Psychology*, 44, 1–11.

This study was carried out in Hamburg, Germany using 120 learners aged 13–14. It was based on a science rubric of five levels that assessed how learners used scientific methods.

Research questions

The investigation was based on a rubric used by teachers for feedback purposes, with a focus to:

- examine the rubric's determining factors of effectiveness

- examine the rubric's possible power in promoting accurate self-judgements, and

- study the relation between external feedback, internal processes of calibration accuracy and performance increase.

Method

The experimental conditions were three conditions of teachers' rubric feedback. In each class, students were randomly divided into the three feedback conditions:

- Condition 1: the rubric to make learning goals transparent (transparency information)

- Condition 2: the rubric and information on the students' actual task performance (individual performance information)

- Condition 3: rubric, actual task performance information, and individual cues on how to proceed (individual performance improvement information).

Data collection

Competence was measured by giving learners the task of writing a scientific experiment for an everyday question that did not require prior scientific knowledge, just the scientific skills being tested. The rubric was used to score their responses.

Motivation was measured by adapting an existing questionnaire (the Intrinsic Motivation Inventory) that asked learners questions about their interest in the subject and their perceived performance in the tasks. This was done before the experiment and after all five tasks were completed.

Learners were asked to predict their score, which was compared to their actual score (calibration accuracy).

Findings

Providing a rubric can improve learning outcomes. However, transparency of learning goals is not enough, as the authors explain (p. 11):

> *Students who received improvement information showed a significantly better performance in planning scientific experiments, perceived themselves as being more competent, and were also more accurate in their self-evaluative performance judgements. This calibration accuracy could be identified to be a partial mediator of the positive effect of rubric feedback on performance. Thus, results indicate that the crucial variable in making teachers' rubric feedback effective appears to be the successful use of performance improvement information.*

Phases towards giving meaningful and effective feedback

Figure 2g2 represents the suggested phases in making lesson objectives effective for fostering a formative assessment culture. Each phase is linked to the practices I will discuss in the rest of this section.

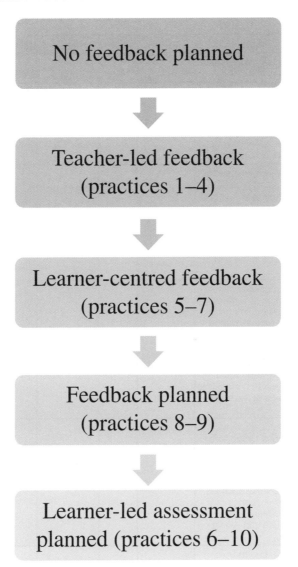

Figure 2g2: Towards giving meaningful and effective feedback

To help you establish which phase you are in and how to develop your practice, use the questionnaire in table 2g1.

Practice analyser: Developing meaningful and effective feedback

Go through the questionnaire (table 2g1) and, for each statement, tick the box that best illustrates your use of that practice.

Table 2g1: Practice analyser: Towards meaningful and effective feedback

	Practice	Regularly	Often	Sometimes	Rarely	Never
1	I mark learners' books with a grade.					
2	I mark learners' books with a grade and comments.					
3	I give learners specific targets as feedback, verbally or in writing.					
4	I give learners specific targets and provide opportunity to respond in lessons.					
5	I use success criteria or rubrics as a method of communicating feedback at the end of a task.					
6	I use success criteria or rubrics as a method of feeding back for improvements during the task.					
7	I use success criteria or rubrics to support learners with providing feedback to themselves or others at the end of a task.					
8	I use success criteria or rubrics to support learners with providing feedback to themselves or others during a task.					
9	Learners use success criteria or rubrics independently to complete and reflect on a task.					
10	Responding to feedback is embedded in my planning, teaching and learners' learning.					

To analyse your results, first identify the best-fit description for your practices. For example, are your responses mostly in the 'rarely' or 'never' categories? If so, you are likely to be in the 'no feedback given' or 'teacher-led feedback' phases, so you would benefit from reading and applying practices 1–4 later in this section. But first, here is some more information on practices and potential next steps.

Analysing your practice and deciding your next steps

Having established the practices you use, decide which practice you would like to develop. Note that the practices at the top of the list are more likely to happen within a classroom with a summative culture, and they get progressively more likely to happen in a formative one. Think about your school assessment culture and your own assessment beliefs and values, so that you can make an achievable next step to improve your classroom assessment practice.

Mostly 'rarely'/'never'

If you do mark books, give general verbal feedback and offer grades as your main form of assessment (practices 1 and 2) then the next steps are to identify some opportunities to try giving specific feedback when marking or in lessons (practice 3) and provide learners with time to respond to that feedback (practice 4). Depending on the culture of your school and classroom, you may wish to start with practices 5, 6, and 7. This will enable you and your learners to develop a more formative, learner-centred culture.

Mostly 'sometimes'

If you sometimes do most of these practices, choose one or two you would like to develop next. Carefully think about your school and classroom culture and consider which practices might benefit you in developing a more formative culture, and improve teaching, learning and assessment in your lessons. Teachers in this situation may want to focus on improving just one practice, such as incorporating or developing success criteria into lessons (practices 5–8), planning opportunities for identifying targets (practice 5), and enabling learners to make improvements (practice 6). Perhaps you could take the use of success criteria a step forward and increase the effectiveness of self-assessment and peer assessment at the end of, or during, a task (practices 7 and 8 respectively). If you want to improve learner independence and self-regulation, consider developing practice 9. Finally, a more ambitious goal may be to plan feedback as a part of every lesson, as discussed in practice 10.

Mostly 'regularly'/'often'

In the case of mostly 'regularly' or 'often' replies, if you have identified a practice that is 'sometimes', perhaps this is the one you may wish to develop, especially if it is lower down the table. Next, if you are already using each of these practices, perhaps you may want to evaluate how effectively you are using them. Reading one of the sections may help you analyse your own implementation and give you new ideas to try and develop.

If you have fully established these practices, then look at another section of Chapter 2 to see what you might like to improve.

 Reflection

Decide on *one* area of your feedback practice that would help improve your classroom assessment. Consider the constraints you have from your school culture and your aspirations for a more formative classroom. Think what is achievable and what is likely to have the most success and impact on teaching, learning and assessment.

- Read the pages that relate to that practice or set of practices.
- Choose one class to trial the activities with.
- Reflect on how your practice has changed and the impact on teaching, learning and assessment.

Marking learners' books with a grade and comments (practices 1 and 2)

Teachers' traditional method of feedback is to 'mark' books or assignments. This is often limited to a few ticks or crosses and a grade. In a summative classroom culture this exists because the teacher is in control of the knowledge and the assessment; the learner has the assessment done to them.

The feedback itself does not have much meaning. Ticks mean correct or good, crosses mean wrong or bad, and, as for the grade, an A is usually good and an F bad, but that is as far as it goes. Often these systems do not have any transparency, and the teacher decides upon grades through experience rather than any objective view.

Towards more formative comments

In my early days of marking books, I often had to put an effort grade as well, to acknowledge a learner's engagement as well as their attainment. This was still summative – something I decided, and it was done to the learners. Often, I would write a lot of managerial comments like 'put the title and date,' 'underline your titles', 'use a ruler for diagrams'. Teachers have mental banks of comments that they write in response to learners' work, but it has been shown that these are not often focused on learning. If I was to change this mental comment bank to be more focused on the learning, I would have a list of comments that I could select and adapt when assessing learners' work.

Later in my teaching, as I was still a bit obsessed with underlined titles, I would get my class to do a quick check and underline any titles before handing in their work. This saved me writing the same – frankly, pointless – comment umpteen times per set of books. Instead, I could focus on using more formative, learning-focused feedback:

- Good graph – write down what it shows.

- Make sure all sentences end with a full stop.

- This is a good description; can you explain why it happened?

- This is a good prediction; can you justify it?

- Explain this in more detail.

- This is a good example of a simile; where else could you use similes?

These examples are focused on skills or learning. They are all intended to identify the next step in learning as decided by the teacher. The teacher draws on their professional knowledge to decide these next steps. Notice that some are written as questions after recognising something good about the work. The example about similes identifies a good model, and encourages greater use of that.

In traditional, more summative, cultures, a step forward is to use comments such as these to improve learning. However, on their own these are not enough. Learners need time to respond to the comments and improve their learning. To set the classroom climate, the teacher needs to use practices that value that. Practices 3 and 4 will help to develop these approaches.

Specific targets as feedback, verbally or in writing (practice 3)

The introduction to this section showed that feedback is best when specific and positive. In a formative classroom culture, teachers need learners to understand what is expected of them, and can achieve this through meaningful objectives and outcomes (sections 2e and 2f).

Figure 2g3 illustrates the effective zone of feedback – where it is specific and positive. Negative and general feedback is not desirable: it can have negative emotional and motivational impact on the learner who receives it.

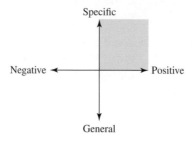

Figure 2g3: What makes feedback effective?

To give examples:

- *Positive and specific feedback*: 'Well done, you have spelled your name correctly. Next time, remember to use a capital letter for the first letter of a sentence.'

- *Negative and general feedback*: 'You can't spell your name. Do it properly next time.'

Teachers can benefit from writing down examples of positive and specific feedback, and evaluating feedback they have given previously.

Meaningful verbal feedback

In one-to-one situations – such as a music teacher tutoring a child at the piano – verbal feedback features heavily. It is often immediate; giving praise, encouragement and next steps. Meaningful verbal feedback can also be achieved with groups of students.

To illustrate this, I want to share with you a physical education lesson I observed at a school in England that teaches learners with special educational needs. The class had eleven learners, who were learning how to trampoline.

The teacher had two learning assistants, one trampoline, and the eleven learners with varying needs (emotional and behavioural difficulties, and moderate to severe learning difficulties). The teacher asked each learner to decide on a target for the lesson that improved on their last trampoline lesson. To enable this, the teacher demonstrated a routine of progressively more challenging types of jump.

The lesson was managed by having all the learners around the trampoline and taking turns at trying their jump. The first learner got on the trampoline and was asked what she was going to attempt. She had three goes at it; each time the teacher gave some tips ('fold your knees sooner', 'face forward', 'bounce higher'). When the learner achieved it, the teacher set a target for her next turn. The next learner had their three attempts. If they did not meet the target, the teacher gave the learner tips for next time. When learners tried their jumps, the teacher would point out a 'model' jump and ask the spectators why they thought it worked.

Every learner had at least three attempts on the trampoline; each knew what they were trying to do and what success looked like, and all made progress based on individual targets. This was all achieved through verbal feedback. The feedback was specific, positive, timely, and achievable, and often the success was modelled. In every case, the learner had a chance to respond to the feedback.

In many classroom situations, often with a ratio of one teacher to thirty or more learners, giving meaningful verbal feedback is more challenging. However, a teacher circulating can give verbal feedback to individual learners or groups of learners, and if a common issue arises, the teacher can address the whole class.

Meaningful written feedback

Teachers traditionally spend hours ticking pages of exercise books using the approach I described in practices 1 and 2. But a variety of strategies can be employed. In written feedback, the same feedback principles apply: specific; positive; timely; and achievable. However, the time needed to write feedback and the value of the feedback have to be balanced. Here I exemplify three strategies to consider how to improve the value and meaning of written feedback.

Identifying strengths and areas for development

The language used should be positive and specific when giving feedback, because it is more likely to motivate the learner to improve. A common approach used in England is the 'WWW and EBI' strategy. At the end of the learner's work the teacher writes the WWW ('what went well') and the EBI ('even better if'). They identify one or two areas of strength next to WWW and areas for improvement for EBI. There are lots of variations on this theme – what is important is that the language is positive and the feedback specific.

Focused written feedback

Using the learning objectives, the teacher can share with the learners that they will only get feedback on a specific area. For example:

- use of verbs in past, present and future tenses

- writing word equations for chemical reactions

- rearranging algebraic equations to change the subject.

The use of success criteria will help communicate what the learner has achieved and what they can do next, for example: 'You have used the present tense accurately. To improve your use of the past and future tenses, you must read textbook pages 23–24, practise with each tense, then correct your work.'

Writing out feedback in this way can take a long time. However, there are some effective short cuts that can be made.

Coded written feedback

When assessing learners' work, teachers will find common, recurring mistakes. They can be listed, coded and shared with students. When the teacher spots the mistake on a learner's work, they write the appropriate code in the margin. At the end of the task, the teacher can select the three most important areas to develop, to make improvements manageable. To ensure that the feedback remains positive, the codes need to be worded positively. Some codes could even be about strengths of the work. An example of this approach is shown in the next classroom case study.

With all these methods, it is important that, once the feedback has been given, learners are given time to read, understand and respond to it. This is discussed in practice 4. To maximise the success of this, learning objectives, learning outcomes, and targets can all be tied together to really focus the feedback, using success criteria or rubrics, as I will show in practices 5 and 6.

Coded marking

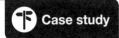 **Case study**

Billy, a secondary English teacher in the UK, described to me how he used marking codes for feedback. He chose numerical codes for areas that were common problems. Billy's marking codes numbers 8–17 were as follows:

- 8. Use the author's surname
- 9. Use terminology
- 10. Link your comments to the question
- 11. Infer, or work out, what the author is saying
- 12. Zoom in on evidence
- 13. Analyse effects of language and/or structure
- 14. Explore alternatives (perhaps)
- 15. Zoom out to comment on theme/context
- 16. Make comparisons
- 17. Write extended answers.

The codes were written on learners' work using a T-grid, identifying a strength and a target. For example, Good use of terminology (9)/Needs to comment on themes or context (15) would look like this:

✓	9
T	15

On receiving back their marked work, Billy encouraged his learners to find the number of the target on the marking code list and to act upon this feedback, guided by a question or instruction to help them to improve their work.

Notice that the feedback is positive and specific. Billy identifies an area of strength and an area for improvement. There are no grades, praise, or other extrinsic motivators – instead, there is complete focus on the task in hand. To go further, Billy could perhaps link tasks, exemplars, or activities to aid learners with their improvements.

Provide targets and the opportunity to respond in lessons (practice 4)

In practices 2 and 3, I have shown how feedback can be communicated positively, specifically, and in a timely manner. However, just providing feedback has limited impact. It does have some, but only the intrinsically motivated learners will respond by taking the feedback on board.

To ensure that all learners understand the feedback you have provided, they need to value the feedback and have time to respond to it. The teacher's role in this is very important. You need to say and show that this process is valued. By setting aside lesson time for learners to respond to your feedback, you will make the learners aware that you value this time. Being clear about your expectations and facilitating the improvement process is also very important. Teachers often express concern about the time taken for making improvements when they could be using the time to teach more content. My argument is that when learners are responding to specific targets, they are actually learning – closing the gap between what they do know and the next steps of what they don't know. Fifteen minutes spent on this type of activity is far more valuable than an hour spent randomly adding ticks to the work.

The teacher can aid the process by providing access to resources that will enable the learners to respond to their feedback targets (see section 2c's classroom case study about a project on household energy efficiency).

Using success criteria or rubrics to communicate feedback (practices 5 and 6)

Having established ways to give verbal and written feedback (practices 1–3), and ways to support the process of learners responding to that feedback, we can look at a more specific strategy of giving feedback during and at the end of a lesson.

Feedback at the end of the lesson (practice 5)

I have discussed in section 2f how to develop tick lists, success criteria, learning ladders and rubrics. These can be used to guide learning and focus assessment throughout the lesson. Teachers often use the end of the lesson to reflect on learning and ascertain next steps in learning. These plenary sessions, when used effectively, allow teachers and learners to understand what has been achieved, and should be able to inform what needs to be done in the next lesson. See also the example of using 'exit tickets' in section 2c.

Digital feedback

Many online schemes of work have quizzes and tests that learners can complete – the computer gives a score and immediate feedback on what to do to improve. In addition, there are a number of mobile phone apps designed for classrooms enabling the teacher to assess the learners' understanding: a question with multiple-choice answers is displayed and the learners select and press a response. The responses are then displayed for the teacher to see how many of the class understand that question.

Although feedback at the end of the lesson has benefits for reflection, metacognition and identification of next steps, it means there is a delay between getting the feedback and having an opportunity to respond. Feedback given during a lesson promotes immediate improvement and self-regulation.

Feedback during the lesson (practice 6)

Feedback during the lesson provides an opportunity for learners to improve. Teacher-led feedback can be difficult to manage in large classes, but not impossible. Smaller classes of around fifteen learners lend themselves more easily to teacher-led feedback. Let's have a look at some strategies.

The structure of the lesson (see section 2c) is important to consider so you can plan time for feedback. This may be while the learners are working – the teacher circulates the classroom, giving feedback – or at a specific moment where the whole class receives feedback.

Feedback is usually best given as immediately as possible. So, planning for a feedback section of the lesson followed by time to improve can be very effective. However, teachers often find it challenging to give feedback to every learner, every lesson. Opportunities for employment of checklists, learning ladders or rubrics can help support each learner to identify where they are now and where they are going, as well as what to do next.

Harnessing mobile apps for immediate feedback

There are many mobile apps now that encourage whole-class involvement and offer individual feedback to the teacher and learners. The following classroom case study describes how a teacher uses such an app in a way that includes developing success criteria.

These strategies foster a much more formative culture, but still have the teacher in control of assessment and feedback. This creates a lot of pressure on the teacher, particularly if feeding back to individuals verbally, or whole classes in writing. To become more formative and allow learners to self-reflect, self-assess and self-regulate their learning, self- and peer assessment are the obvious next steps (practices 7 and 8).

Using mobile apps for feedback

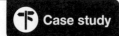 **Case study**

Thomas experimented with an application called *GoFormative*. The app allows teachers to monitor every student and give instant feedback as students work through a digitised worksheet. The app helps with spotting misconceptions and resolving them immediately. Because teachers can see every piece of work being written they can ensure every single student has addressed the misconception and made progress. It's also very effective for helping students improve the structure of their answers. Thomas said:

> *What I'd usually do is monitor the responses until I find one that I can use as a model for the rest of the class. Then, I'd project this onto the whiteboard and we'd discuss what is good about the answer and then develop a set of success criteria that the students could use to improve their own responses, using the answers. Throughout all of this, I am monitoring their responses, intervening where necessary to give encouragement, prompt and challenge students. As such, in terms of differentiation, it's also a very powerful tool. Also, every time I have used the app, even with the trickiest of classes, within minutes the students are engrossed, and the only sound in the air is the pleasant rapid clicking of keyboards.*

This is an example of where digital applications can support the teacher with formative assessment, even with longer pieces of work. From what Thomas says, we can see that he holds formative values and uses modelling, whole-class strategies, and individual intervention to help all learners learn.

Using success criteria and rubrics for feedback in self- and peer assessment (practices 7 and 8)

These practices have strong connections to section 2h and draw on some of the key ideas discussed there.

Learner-led at end of task (practice 7)

Such feedback can be effective and meaningful if the learners have been provided with the success criteria at the start of the task; the teacher has taken time to model and develop meaning with the class; and the teacher plans time for self-assessment or peer assessment at the end of the lesson.

Either the learners can assess their own work or swap work to peer assess (see section 2h) using the success criteria. The teacher needs to provide enough time so that the process is not rushed – the learners have to see the value of identifying strengths and areas for development. Although this is useful at the end of the lesson, it can create a summative assumption, as there is no opportunity to respond to the feedback. The focus of the lesson is on the outcome, not necessarily the process. This approach is even better if there is a formative moment within the lesson itself.

Learner-led during task (practice 8)

Reminding learners regularly to check their progress against the success criteria you have given them can help focus the learning process and enhance formative values. Planning a formal moment within the lesson for all learners to do either a quick self-assessment or peer assessment can ensure that all learners know what they have achieved so far and confirm their next steps.

Once learners are practising good habits of using success criteria they can start to work independently, confidently and self-regulate – practice 9.

Learners use success criteria or rubrics independently (practice 9)

I have been arguing for developing independent, self-reflecting, self-regulating learners as a major goal for education beyond learning subject content. Modelling the meaningful feedback practices I've described could lead to some classes becoming self-regulating.

Learners will ask for the success criteria, or develop it themselves when given a task. They will discuss what success might look like. They will apply this knowledge to the task in hand: regularly checking they are on track, problem-solving, collaborating, and asking for help when they are really stuck. They will then be able to talk confidently about their achievements and next steps. Maybe then your work as a teacher is done!

Responding to feedback is embedded in planning (practice 10)

Once you are confident with the practices you have developed, you will want to plan them into your lessons more regularly, and embed a formative feedback culture where improvement is valued over outcome. Section 2c shows some models for planning classroom assessment and helps you to embed meaningful feedback.

How to

When planning your lessons, ensure that you make time for feedback, using these principles.

Feedback should be:

- frequent and detailed
- positive and specific
- focused on the learner's performance or learning, not personal characteristics
- timely
- linked to shared criteria
- appropriate and accessible to the learner
- addressed by the teacher and learner
- acted upon by the learner.

2h) Meaningful self- and peer assessment

This section considers how teachers can include self- and peer assessment in their classroom. This is probably one of the most culturally challenging aspects of classroom assessment practice. When done effectively, however, it develops unique skills for learners, not just in assessment, but social and professional skills as well.

The kind of 'peer assessment' I often see taking place in classrooms reflects my own experience as a schoolboy. In spelling tests, for example, the teacher would read out ten words and I would write these down, using (hopefully) the correct spellings. Then I would swap my paper with the person next to me. The teacher would read out the correct spellings and we would mark each other's as either correct or incorrect.

In this section, I will argue that peer assessment has so much more potential than this very basic approach suggests. Self-assessment and peer assessment are, arguably, the most difficult forms of assessment to get right, but when a teacher does, the benefits are unique and potentially enormous.

The three types of assessment we consider in this book are teacher assessment, learner self-assessment and learner peer assessment. I define these as:

- *Teacher assessment:* the process of a teacher responding to learners' work, making educational judgements and feeding back, often with the support of a mark scheme or success criteria.

- *Self-assessment*: the process of a learner making educational judgements on their own work and identifying improvements, often with the support of a mark scheme or success criteria.

- *Peer assessment*: the process of a learner making educational judgements on another learner's work and identifying improvements, often with the support of a mark scheme or success criteria.

The culture of teachers and assessment

The practices for self- and peer assessment require considerable cultural shifts from assessment in traditional classrooms. In most cultures, the teacher is seen as the assessor of work; their judgement is usually respected, and learners and their parents hold the teacher's feedback in high esteem. A teacher relinquishing their responsibility for assessing work to the learner – or worse, another learner in the class – can cause cultural shock waves.

Teachers take pride in being accurate and reliable assessors. Most see it as their job to mark books and to give feedback on work, effort and behaviour. It requires a shift in teachers' beliefs and attitudes to take on these more learner-focused practices.

The teacher needs heightened cultural awareness to help change beliefs and attitudes of colleagues, learners and parents. To do this, the strategies used for self- and peer assessment have to be introduced with care, transparency, and awareness of the pitfalls.

In many classrooms, I have seen teachers ask a few questions as a quick quiz to check knowledge and understanding. The learners then self-assess; that is, mark their own work, as the teacher offers the correct answers. There are some underlying assumptions here: the quiz is not seen as high value; it's just a quick knowledge check; it has no bearing on your final grade. The teacher is fully in control of the knowledge; they call out the questions and the correct answers. The learner just has to recall the answers and then check they are correct. The assessment culture is summative. However, the learner is trusted to mark accurately and not cheat.

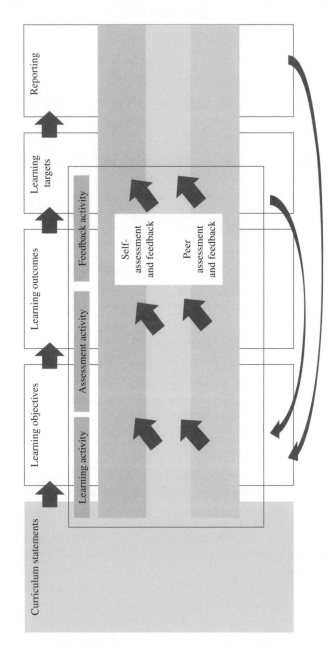

Figure 2h1: A model for classroom assessment: Where self- and peer assessment fit in

A similar, but peer-marked quiz (like my primary school spelling tests) seems to have further underlying assumptions: the spelling test is slightly more important (the teacher used to record our scores in his mark book) and a peer is given the responsibility to mark the test to ensure learners do not cheat.

Self- and peer assessment are so much more than the learners doing the teacher's job for them. However, to have success with these, it is important to clarify the specific purpose of self- and peer assessment, use strategies that optimise effectiveness, and support learners in the process of becoming good at some assessment practices and feedback.

Where self- and peer assessment fit in the classroom assessment model

The teacher needs to have cultural and social awareness to create appropriate conditions to support learners in developing self- and peer assessment skills. It will take time, but once the skills have been acquired, they have lifelong value and offer unique opportunities in effective learning.

These approaches are effective at allowing learners to assess and improve their work, bridging the assessment activity and feedback activity, and generating appropriate learning targets, which feed back to the learning objectives and outcomes, either during the lesson or in a subsequent lesson (figure 2h1).

Phases towards more learner-focused assessment

I have constructed a framework through which I illustrate the phases of self- and peer assessment in the classroom (figure 2h2). It is by no means perfect or prescriptive, but simply a guide. These phases move in general from summative assumptions to more formative ones. However, in all cases, it's not what you do, but the way that you do it.

 Also see

This section builds on practices introduced in sections:

- 2c) Planning meaningful assessment
- 2g) Giving meaningful and effective feedback

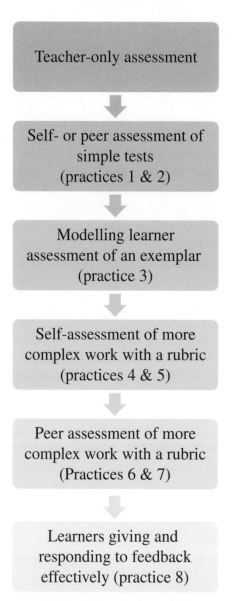

Figure 2h2: Towards meaningful self-assessment and peer assessment

Purposes and benefits of self-assessment and peer assessment

The educational research into self- and peer assessment in the classroom is in relative infancy – we are still in the process of understanding the full benefits, effective processes and pitfalls associated with this aspect of classroom assessment. However, we do know that the purposes of self- and peer assessment are multifaceted, because they:

- shift the responsibility for, and trust in, assessment from teacher to learner

- increase learner engagement and application of assessment or success criteria

- create opportunities for self-reflection and metacognition

- create opportunities for peer interaction and learning from each other

- increase confidence in the important aspects of learning

- develop interpersonal skills of sensitively feeding back

- promote self-correction

- develop self-regulated learners.

Towards a self-regulated learner

Self-regulation as a life skill is probably one of the most important that education can offer. It means having awareness of how well you are doing, and a skill set to make adjustments towards a goal. We self-regulate it on a basic scale in everyday life – for example, when washing the dishes, I sometimes clean too quickly and miss parts of a plate, or forget to wash the underside. When I notice my mistakes, I go back and correct them, sometimes with exasperation, but nonetheless I am self-regulating. In more complex tasks such as writing a report, constructing a building, or managing a meeting, the skills of self-regulation become very important.

Self-assessment is an essential skill for a self-regulated learner. It models the process of knowing what you are trying to achieve, checking you are achieving it, identifying gaps in your own knowledge and understanding, and responding to those observations. The set of sub-skills within this includes self-reflection, metacognition and self-correction:

- *Self-reflection* is the skill of considering your own actions and behaviour. In this context, it can be associated with a learner reflecting how they feel about a particular activity; for example, how difficult they found it, whether it was interesting, how well they think they did and the reasons for this.

- *Metacognition* is the skill of reflecting on *how* you have learned something. For example, a learner may be able to reflect upon how they tackled something they found difficult.

- *Self-correction* is the ability of a learner to assess their own progress against an expectation (model or success criteria) and adjust to improve their performance.

The special features of peer assessment

The nature of peer interaction is of particular interest, as it appears to have unique benefits to learning. For me, some of the most revealing research was conducted by the late Professor Graham Nuthall. His key findings are summarised in *The Hidden Lives of Learners*,[51] a book that changed my perspective on how much learning takes place between learners in the classroom. (Nuthall's insights about examination systems also inform my thinking in Chapter 3.)

Based in New Zealand, Nuthall conducted many experiments during the 1990s and 2000s, focusing on the behaviour in the classroom (learning and otherwise) of individual learners and between learners. Of particular interest is what Nuthall calls 'private talk to self and peers,' where he recorded and analysed what learners say to themselves and each other while a lesson is in progress. Although not specifically looking at assessment, Nuthall's research shows that much of what learners learn in the classroom comes from their peers. From this premise he argues that teachers must foster a culture that allows peer interactions to enhance learning outcomes.

Part of this, I contend, is the use of self- and peer assessment strategies. These are so much more than achieving an 'accurate' assessment of a piece of work; instead they should foster independence in learning and, particularly, self-regulation. The focus of these approaches is not so much on accurate knowledge – although that is desirable – but on skills of evaluation, interpersonal interaction (giving feedback effectively and kindly), and engaging with and applying success criteria.

Student-led assessment and feedback

In section 2g I described our current understanding of the giving and receiving of effective feedback in the classroom. Much of this can be used when considering how we support learners to assess their own work and that of others. To recap briefly – feedback should be: frequent and detailed; positive and specific; focused on the learners' performance or learning, not personal characteristics; timely; linked to shared criteria; appropriate and accessible to the learner; addressed by the teacher and learner; and acted upon by the learner.

---

[51] **G. Nuthall** (2007). *The Hidden Lives of Learners*. Wellington: NZCER Press.

Student self-assessment

This research case study is based on a very large-scale investigation of primary and secondary school learners in Hong Kong. It looks specifically at self-assessment using two psychological domains. First, two types of self-assessment practice: 'feedback seeking' and 'self-reflection.' Second, the two types of motivation: extrinsic ('performance-goal oriented') and intrinsic ('mastery-goal oriented'). Extrinsically motivated learners focus on outcomes, grades and praise, whereas intrinsically motivated learners focus on mastering the task itself, and are motivated by the process of learning.

Yan, Z. (2016). Student self-assessment practices: the role of gender, school level and goal orientation. *Assessment in Education: Principles, Policy & Practice*, August 2016, 1–17.

A total of 8843 primary (ages 9–11) and secondary (ages 12–18) students responded to a paper-and-pencil questionnaire.

Research questions

1. Are there differences regarding self-assessment practice (self-directed feedback seeking and self-reflection) across gender and school levels?

2. Is there a relationship between goal orientation (mastery-goal oriented and performance-goal oriented) and self-assessment practice (self-directed feedback seeking and self-reflection) among primary and secondary school students?

Findings

Female students in both primary and secondary demonstrated (statistically significant) higher levels of self-assessment practices than male students. This finding supports several other studies that show that females are better than males at most aspects of self-assessment.

Older students are less likely to engage in self-assessment practices, with the difference in self-reflection being statistically significant. This is at odds with studies in Western cultures.

Implications

- Teachers should find ways to encourage and facilitate student self-assessment, especially for male learners.

- Learners in 'exam years' may undervalue self-assessment practices, focusing instead on quick-gain learning strategies.

Feedback by self- and peer assessment can provide many, if not all, of these opportunities, along with the development of some skills that only self- or peer assessment can provide.

Developing meaningful self-assessment and peer assessment

Have a go at evaluating your own practice. In the table below, decide how often you do these practices with a particular class. Do not overthink, just respond to each statement. Then use the guidance underneath to decide on your next steps for using self-assessment and peer assessment in your lessons.

To analyse your results, first identify the best-fit description for your practices. For example, are your responses mostly in the 'rarely' or 'never' categories? If so, you are likely to be in the 'teacher assessment' or 'self- or peer marking of simple tests' phases, so you would benefit from reading and applying practices 1–4. But first, here is some more information on practices and potential next steps.

Table 2h1: Practice analyser: Developing meaningful self-assessment and peer assessment

	Practice	Always	Often	Sometimes	Rarely	Never
1	I give my learners quizzes/ tests to self-assess (mark themselves) in lessons.					
2	I give my learners quizzes/ tests to peer assess (mark each other's) in lessons.					
3	I give my learners exemplar work to show desired outcomes.					
4	I am confident with supporting my learners to self-assess their work effectively.					
5	I give my learners rubrics or success criteria to assess their own work.					
6	I am confident with supporting my learners to peer assess work.					
7	I give my learners rubrics or success criteria to assess each other's work.					
8	I plan lessons so there is time for learners to improve their work after it is peer or self-assessed.					

Analysing your practice and deciding your next steps

Having established the practices you use, decide which practice you would like to develop. Note that the practices at the top of the list are more likely to happen in a classroom with a summative assessment culture and they get progressively more likely to be found in a formative one. Think also about the school's assessment culture and your assessment beliefs and values so you can make an achievable next step to improve your classroom assessment practice.

Mostly 'rarely'/'never'

If you only do teacher assessment at the moment, the next step is to try some simple self- and peer assessment of closed-question tests (practices 1 and 2). These will help you gain confidence to hand over some responsibility to learners and to reflect on their engagement with this style of assessment. The learners will also go through a shift in understanding your expectations and the benefits of doing assessment in this way.

Note that you must ensure that you have introduced some of the other assessment approaches first, such as the development of effective success criteria and rubrics (section 2f), effective methods of feeding back, and responding effectively to feedback (section 2g).

Mostly 'sometimes'

If you sometimes do most of these practices, choose one or two you would like to develop next. Carefully think about your school and classroom culture and consider which practices might benefit you in developing a more formative culture and improve teaching, learning and assessment in your lessons. Teachers in this situation may want to focus on improving just one practice, such as the use of exemplars (practice 3), supporting self-assessment of more complex assignments (4 and 5), or supporting peer assessment of more complex assignments (6 and 7).

Mostly 'regularly'/'often'

In the case of mostly 'regularly'/'often', if you have identified a practice that is 'sometimes', perhaps this is the one you may wish to develop, especially if it is lower down the table. Next, if you are already using each of these practices, you may want to evaluate how effectively you are using them. Reading one of the sections may help you analyse your implementation and give you new ideas to try and develop.

Reflection

Decide on *one* area of practice in self- and peer assessment that would help improve your classroom assessment. Consider the constraints you have from your school culture and your own aspirations for a more formative classroom. Think what is achievable and what is likely to have the most success and impact on teaching, learning and assessment.

- Read the pages that relate to that practice or set of practices.
- Choose one class to trial the activities with.
- Reflect on how your practice has changed and the impact on teaching, learning and assessment.

If you have fully established these practices, then look at another section of Chapter 2 to see what you might like to improve.

How to develop shared values in learner-led assessment (practices 1–8)

Depending on the experience and culture of the class, you may need to introduce self- and peer assessment explicitly. Sharing your expectations, what success looks like, and the ground rules will help manage the situation. It will give you the opportunity to praise adherence to the expectations and remind those who stray from the guidelines, thus reinforcing the expectations.

Explain your expectations, such as these:

- I am going to give you responsibility to have a go at assessing a piece of work: [an exemplar/your own/another's].

- Use the [information/mark scheme/criteria] to inform your judgement.

- Don't worry if you are not certain of your judgement – use the [information/mark scheme/criteria] to justify your judgement.

- The purpose of this is to help you make evidence-based judgements, and provide useful feedback respectfully.

- Take the opportunity to learn by making improvements to your own work and learning from others.

- Take regular opportunities to praise and reinforce these expectations verbally or in writing.

How to do self- or peer assessment of simple tests (practices 1 and 2)

If you currently do not use any learner-led assessment, the following is a useful stepping stone to shifting assessment responsibility from teacher to learner. The approach can be introduced as a quiz or a test that consists of a few (no more than ten) closed questions. These could be spellings, factual recall or mental arithmetic. The teacher simply reads out each question and the learners write down their answers. The teacher then reads out the answers and the learners mark their own answers. Alternatively, the learners can swap papers and mark each other's.

Traditionally, teachers might collect the marks achieved. I have previously got learners to raise their hand if they got a particular score ('less than five out of ten', 'six correct', 'seven correct', and so on). Those learners who got half or more incorrect will require extra help, but often this is overlooked; the focus is on the final score and the quiz is delivered with summative assumptions. So, a next step could be to make the quiz more formative.

Reflecting on learning

Instead of focusing on what the learners got right, develop a more formative process by giving the learners five minutes to respond to questions such as those suggested below. The questions can be written or displayed on the board, or provided on a slip of paper with space for their responses. Alternatively, learners can ask a peer the questions and compare answers. This will start the process of peer discussion and move towards peer assessment opportunities.

Questions for learners after marking their quiz

- Which questions did you get wrong?
- Why did you get them wrong?
- Do you know the correct answer now?
- If so, do you understand the answer?
- What have you learned from doing this quiz?

Deciding on feedback

The learners may need some guidance on how to answer these reflective questions. The first few times, you may need to coach learners to understand how and why they are reflecting. To do this, the teacher's role is to increase the value of the reflection and feedback over the need for grades, to ensure that learners will come to understand and value the process. Here are some suggested questions and interventions.

- What are the reasons that you got [a particular answer] wrong?
    - You didn't revise?
    - You missed that lesson?
    - You didn't understand the question?
    - You didn't understand the answer?
    - You made a mistake?
- What can you do to learn and understand the answer?
    - Find a way to memorise that spelling, factoid, or process.
    - Do some exercises or practise to learn the missing knowledge.
    - Do some research and rework the knowledge to make meaning.

The teacher may need to facilitate the learners in finding suitable techniques and resources to do these improvement practices. For example: recommend the 'look-cover-write-check' method for spelling; direct learners to some exercises in a textbook to do some practice questions; and use mind maps or other methods for reworking knowledge to make new meanings.

Responding to feedback

If the quiz is designed so that most learners can achieve all the marks, teachers may want to match up those who achieved all the answers with those who did not. This encourages peer learning, where the learner that needs help can get that help from a peer – and the peer will gain experience from teaching another learner through having to explain and justify the correct answers.

The limitation of this method is that the teacher is very much in control of the knowledge and the assessment process. By changing the focus of the quiz from outcome to process – summative to formative – it does start to develop some shared values of a formative culture, but the learners are still having the assessment done to them.

How to model learner assessment with an exemplar (practice 3)

Before starting an assignment such as a piece of writing, an investigation, or a painting, the use of an exemplar or exemplars can encourage learners to explore opportunities and pitfalls.

In my spare time, I like drawing and painting flowers and insects. To do this, I often start with a photograph that I have taken, but I also search the Internet for other paintings of that type of flower or insect. I evaluate the online paintings, searching for techniques that work and those to avoid. By doing this, I learn from others and can integrate ideas and techniques into my own attempt. Encouraging learners to follow the same process will help them to make decisions and have the best opportunities at being successful in their assignment.

Using exemplars with an assessment rubric can be a useful stepping stone towards more independent self-assessment and peer assessment practices. Exemplars can take various forms including:

- examples of the type of writing, a similar investigation, or images that can be used as inspiration and have a rubric applied

- anonymised examples of the same or similar assignment from another class

- examples mocked up by the teacher to exemplify the key characteristics of the assignment.

Using exemplar material in an art lesson 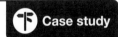 Case study

An approach to engaging learners with the process can be exemplified by this class of 12–13-year-olds doing an art lesson focused on pencil drawings using shade, form and texture. The teacher has provided three sketches of a vase of dried flowers. These sketches were done by learners in other classes in the same year group. The pictures were anonymised and labelled as sketches A, B and C. At the start of the lesson, the teacher provides the class with the rubric that describes the criteria for different levels of success when focusing on the features of shade, form and texture in pencil drawings.

Copies of the three exemplar drawings are given to small groups of learners and they are instructed to look at each one and use the rubric to assess them. The teacher gives the students five minutes to assess each sketch.

She tells them to identify features of the sketches that meet the criteria on the rubrics.

After this session, the teacher asks the learners to give their assessment of each sketch, based on the rubric. The type of response is generally in keeping with what the teacher expects, but where there are differences the teacher helps develop the discussion. For example, the texture in sketch A is very detailed and varies between the different types of flowers, while that in sketch C is less distinct. However, two groups assess sketch C as having better texture than sketch A. When the teacher explores this, she finds that one group of learners thought that texture was to do with 'neatness', had seen sketch C as neater, and therefore thought it had better texture. The teacher could correct this misunderstanding, and the learners learned what the rubric meant when referring to texture. The second group think that the vase in sketch A didn't have enough texture and go on to discuss whether smoothness is itself a texture – again learning.

After discussing which features of each sketch were drawn well, the teacher gives the groups the opportunity to discuss techniques they would try when they do their own sketches of a similar still life. She asks them to write down one aspect they would aim for in each of the three categories: form, shade and texture. When the learners start their own sketches they have a better idea of what they are trying to achieve.

The advantage of using anonymised exemplars was that the learners paid attention just to the drawings and not any personal or social issues. The grading itself was not prioritised; instead, the teacher used the learner assessment to understand exactly what the learners understood by the rubric criteria. By doing this, the learners grew more confident at interpreting the criteria and became more comfortable with assessing their own work and that of others.

Note that the culture of the classroom is more formative; valuing the process over the outcome – that is exactly what the sketchers had done and what the learners were going to do. The assessment process of applying the rubric was used to inform learning, so the learners were very much part of the assessment process, with clear, shared expectations. The teacher ensured they understood the expectations through questioning, and allowed them to make mistakes and make progress. I can imagine the learners applying the criteria at the end of the lesson to their own sketches, or even each other's work.

Reflection

Thinking about exemplars:

- What type of exemplar material could you use in your subject?
- How could you use it to exemplify the success criteria of an assignment?

Once you have tried this approach:

- What learning opportunities took place when learners assessed the exemplars?
- Did the exercise have any impact on the success of the learners' own work?
- What barriers or difficulties did you face? How might you avoid or address these in future?

How to do self-assessment with more complex work with a rubric (practices 4 and 5)

Before learners can self-assess effectively, a teacher needs to be able to support them. This requires skill and confidence in formative practices, including the development of effective success criteria and rubrics (section 2f), plus effective methods of feeding back and responding effectively to feedback (2g). Remember also that learners will not be able to achieve success at this immediately. You will need to plan regular opportunities for learners to experience self-assessment (perhaps once a week) and develop their skills and confidence in the process.

Supporting self-assessment

Look at this section's research case study and you will see that Zi Yan has some clear advice about supporting self-assessment. To enable self-assessment to be effective, teachers should provide: clear assessment criteria; models of self-assessment; opportunities for self-assessment; and highlight successful past experiences in self-assessment.[52]

If the learners have already experienced assessment of exemplar material (practice 3) they will be more confident and equipped with the skills to understand and apply the success criteria. The exemplar approach allows the teacher to model self-assessment and demonstrate how to become a reflective learner. I would add that the teacher needs to be very clear about the expectations of the assessment process from the start, letting the class know that part of the assessment will be a self-assessment and explaining what that means.

---

[52] **Z. Yan**, *Assessment in Education: Principles, Policy & Practice*, August 2016.

Even without clear learning criteria and success criteria, some simple questions at the end of an assignment – before it is submitted for teacher assessment – can help learners be more reflective:

- *What do you think you did well? Why?*
- *Which aspect are you most proud of? Why?*
- *What would you do differently next time?*
- *If you had five more minutes [/an extra day/other appropriate timeframe] what would you do next?*

If learners are provided with assessment criteria at the start of the assignment, the questions could be more specific.

Using the success criteria/rubric:

- *Which parts of your assignment are the strongest? Why?*
- *Which parts could be better? Why?*
- *Which parts could you improve? How?*

When to self-assess

Instead of doing the self-assessment at the end of the assignment, plan to do it part way through the work and use the exercise to make improvements to the ongoing work before it is submitted. Alternatively, have drafting as part of an assignment and self-assess the draft against the success criteria, then allow learners to use the feedback to improve their own learning and final assignment.

Pitfalls

By setting clear expectations there will be fewer issues, but learners unaccustomed to these practices can sometimes stray from the desired behaviours. Specific issues to be aware of and challenge are negative comments, mocking behaviour and sarcasm. Remind learners to concentrate on the work and the criteria it is being assessed against. Identify the positive and the next steps. It is important that teachers take time to train learners in these feedback skills, as detailed in section 2g.

Support for all learners

A number of research papers have shown that male learners are less likely to engage with self-reflection than female learners. This means that the teacher needs to put in extra support, exemplification and discussion to encourage some male learners to engage with the activity and maximise the benefits.

In addition, learners with special educational needs may need this process adapted. Simple self-assessment approaches can use basic criteria and sad, neutral and smiley face symbols as indictors of how well something has been achieved.

Learners not understanding the purpose

Some learners may take time to see the point of self-assessment and peer assessment. This will only be remedied through experience. However, there are number of actions the teacher can take to help learners overcome their scepticism. These include the explicit sharing of the types of benefits expected, drawing the whole class's attention to moments where particular learners have self-assessed their work successfully and are using feedback well, and using exemplars of benefits to learning and success in an assignment.

Learners being too harsh or too generous

This is not unique to learners – as we know, teachers face the same issue. Therefore, when a learner is too harsh on themselves ('this isn't very good, is it?'), counter it with 'what are the best bits?' and 'which bits could you improve?' Encourage them to compare their work with the criteria carefully, taking each statement to assess one at a time.

Conversely, a learner may think their work meets all the criteria and there is nothing left for them to do. In this case, the criteria may need improving to extend everyone in the class. More likely, the learner has not engaged with the criteria. So, breaking down the success criteria and exemplifying which parts of their work best meet these will help them become more involved with the assessment process.

Peer assessment of more complex work with a rubric (practices 6 and 7)

Peer assessment, arguably, has more complexities and challenges than self-assessment, not least the development of trust between peers. It can feel exposing to allow a peer to assess (especially if it is someone the learner does not know well). It can also feel uncomfortable and exposing if this is done in a culture where outcomes are valued more than processes. So teachers need to introduce this practice sensitively, being clear about expectations and reminding learners who stray.

Supporting peer assessment

Features of successful peer assessment were summarised by educational researcher Sarah Gielen and her colleagues in Belgium.[53] They concluded that

---

[53] **S. Gielen, E. Peeters, F. Dochy, P. Onghena & K. Struyven** (2010). Improving the effectiveness of peer feedback for learning. *Learning and Instruction*, 20(4), 304–315.

successful peer assessment required: shared success criteria; opportunity for assessment by a peer and many peers; learners trained in peer assessment; learners trained in providing feedback; and teacher support for the peer assessment process.

Notice that there are two features that require learners to be trained in the activity. Peer assessment is not an easy activity. It requires several skills, including the ability to use and understand success criteria and, from that, decide upon effective feedback. Alongside that are the social skills required to deliver feedback sensitively.

 Reflection

Think how you might develop self-assessment and peer assessment practices:

- Which class(es) might respond well to this approach? Why?
- Which topic, assignment or work during the assignment might lend itself to learner assessment?
- What models of the process might you use with the learners?
- How will you demonstrate your expectations of this type of assessment?
- What benefits will you communicate with them?
- What pitfalls do you anticipate, and how might you support learners to avoid these?

Managing the social aspects of peer assessment

The teacher needs to manage the social situation with care and sensitivity. As learners become more familiar with the process and confident in their own use of criteria, they will become more self-regulating and independent. You can set the classroom climate for peer assessment by providing learners with prompts. Prompts for assessing another learner's work include:

- What did they do well and why?
- What didn't they do well and why?
- If I were you I would... Maybe you could...
- It would even be better if you...
- Your best part is... because...
- This time I paid special attention to... because...

How to support learners giving and responding to feedback (practice 8)

Giving and responding to feedback is a skill that needs to be learned. Here I identify some examples of how to encourage learners to develop these skills.

Deciding on feedback

Deciding on feedback is challenging enough for teachers. Many a time have I agonised over the exact phrase to use when providing feedback. With more experience, I have become more confident in tentatively asking the learner for feedback and then helping them to refine it, often referring back to the

---

Whole-class peer assessment 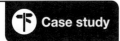 **Case study**

The learners have each created a shoebox model that shows patterns in the solar system. At the start of the assignment, the learners are given the success criteria and know that they will have their work peer assessed. The success criteria are presented in a rubric (table 2h2).[54]

Once completed, the models are displayed around the classroom. The learners are then given sticky notes. Learners will each visit three models (assigned by random) and assess them using the rubric. They are instructed to make the following judgements:

- What you have done well

- Why I think this

- What you could improve

- What I learned from your model (or a question for the model maker).

The learners write their comments on the sticky note, add their name, and stick the note to the model they have assessed. At the end of the session, each model will have several sticky notes with formative comments attached. Learners can read the comments and decide upon a few areas they would improve on.

---

[54]**A. Grevatt & V. Stutt** (2009). *Physics Homework Tasks with Learning Ladders*. Stevenage: Badger Publishing.

Table 2h2: Level ladder for solar system shoebox project, adapted by permission of Badger Publishing Ltd.

	The types of things you can do
Advanced	You will have *made a detailed solar system shoebox model*, drawing on detailed scientific knowledge and understanding. • Explain how you have calculated the scale of your model. • Explain in detail, and compare, what each planet and its orbit is like. • Explain in detail how we know information about the planets and further exploration that could take place about the solar system.
Confident	You will have *made a solar system shoebox model*, drawing on scientific knowledge and understanding. • Accurately represent the size and distance of the planets, approximately to scale. • Explain what each planet is like and how they remain in orbit. • Explain how we know information about the planets.
Establishing	You will have *made a simple solar system shoebox model*, drawing on some scientific knowledge and understanding. • Represent the planets in the correct order, with roughly correct sizes of each planet used. • Describe and show what each planet is like. • State some ways information has been found out about the planets in the past.

rubric or learning outcomes. The conversations are probably a valuable learning experience in themselves because this models self-regulation, the application of a rubric, clarifies terminology, and helps define the gap between the learner's current work and the ideal.

Responding to feedback: improving the work

As discussed in section 2g, feedback and the opportunity to respond to it are essential for effective learning. Planning time for learner responses to the feedback (section 2c) is essential for closing the feedback loop. Giving time within the lesson will show the learners that you value improvements to their work and the value of responding to feedback.

Tips for encouraging a formative culture

This should be encouraged as a two-way process – not only do learners give feedback, they learn from the models as well. If this is the first time, you may want to ensure that learners only offer positive comments, so discuss how to phrase and deliver comments that are positive and formative.

I have used this process by having coloured sticky notes. Green notes are positive comments, yellow are for a question and pink are formative suggestions. By doing this, the assessor has a focus and the learner who has been assessed can see which comments are positive, which are formative, and which need answering.

It sometimes helps to have a rubric with suggested sentence starters to encourage learners to provide constructive feedback:

- I like part... because it shows/explains/describes/presents... idea clearly/well/cleverly.

- I would like to have more information about part...

- Can you explain part... more clearly/further by adding an example?

- Have you thought about presenting section... as a table/diagram/chart/graph?

 How to

Self-assessment and peer assessment promote unique opportunities to learn how to self-reflect and self-regulate, and to give and receive feedback. This can be achieved through:

- providing clear assessment criteria

- planning opportunities for self-assessment and peer assessment

- modelling self-assessment and peer assessment

- providing scaffolds, prompts and structures through which to decide upon and react to feedback

- highlighting successful past experiences in self-assessment and peer assessment.

2i) Using summative tests, formatively

Tests and exams are deeply engrained in education systems around the world, and their language ('making the grade') is part of our culture. The end of secondary education is seen as the pinnacle for all learners to be examined and get grades that will determine their future success, or lack of it.[55]

The Chinese are credited with inventing the examination. In the short time I have spent in Beijing, I observed a noticeable reliance on written examinations and certification. Developing countries like Kazakhstan have invested heavily in developing a world-leading examination system that allows them to be competitive in the global arena. When talking to learners in its high schools, many of them have high expectations of themselves and see good grades as synonymous with their success in life. The UK has a system of comparison and judgement of schools known as 'league tables', based on the number of learners that achieve certain grades. This has been refined by looking not only at grades, but also at improvement over the learner's school career.

So far, I have talked about 'high-stakes' assessment. These are usually national examinations that are related to qualifications. These are perceived as having high value, and are used as a way of discerning which applicant is suitable for a job or entry to other qualifications.

Forms of testing

Here are definitions of terms I will use in this section.

Examinations: usually high stakes and produced and marked externally from the school. These are used to award qualifications. Past exam papers can be used in schools as mock exams and to model the styles of question to expect.

Tests: usually low stakes, used to test knowledge, understanding and skills after a short episode of learning. Often created and used by teachers to check on what learners have learned. These can become higher stakes if used to make decisions based on learners' progress in school, such as changing classes.

Quizzes: often brief tests used to quickly check knowledge, understanding and skills. These are low stakes, as no summative decision about a learner's performance is made.

---

[55]**W. Mansell** (2007). *Education by Numbers: The Tyranny of Testing*. London: Politico's Publishing.

As I explained in section 2a, it's 'not what you do, but the way that you do it'. This is no different with examinations, tests and quizzes. Teachers can choose how to use summative assessments as formatively as possible.

It is worth noting that, in this context, I am dealing with tests and examinations that are part of the classroom assessment system. There are many types of test, with a range of purposes; not all are suitable, or worthwhile, to use in a formative way.

Psychological studies show that low-stakes testing and self-testing can have huge benefits in retaining information, knowledge and facts. In the form of low-stakes quizzes and online tests that only the learner uses to check their knowledge, understanding and skills, instant feedback can have beneficial effects. Another benefit is the opportunity to re-test the learning after a period of time has elapsed, known as *interleaving*.[56]

Although the system of testing is deeply encultured, there is growing concern over whether assessment through testing and examinations is fit for purpose in the modern age. Paul Black discussed some of the issues associated with tests and testing in his book *Testing: Friend or Foe?*,[57] which recognises the uses of different types of test but highlights what he calls the 'rocky road' of obstacles that need to be considered when using them. More recently, Gordon Stobart, a professor in Education based in the UK, explores similar territory in his book *Testing Times: The Uses and Abuses of Assessment*. Stobart contends a similar argument to mine, that 'assessment shapes how we see ourselves as learners and as people',[58] and offers a series of steps to reclaiming assessment.

One of the most pertinent issues associated with giving learners grades is that learners start to build their identity based on their grades. Learners can be defined by their grades. For learners who are successful in the examination system, this can lead to them becoming reliant on grades and hugely disappointed if they ever fail to meet the top grade. This can lead to mental health issues associated with their identity and academic success and an inability to deal with failure. Learners who are less successful in the academic system can become demotivated; defined as stupid, not intelligent, or, as one paper reports, self-identified as 'a nothing'.[59]

---

[56] **D. Rohrer** (2012). Interleaving helps students distinguish among similar concepts. *Educational Psychology Review*, 24, 355–367.

[57] **P. Black** (1998). *Testing: Friend or Foe? Theory and Practice of Assessment and Testing*. Oxon: RoutledgeFalmer.

[58] **G. Stobart** (2008). *Testing Times: The Uses and Abuses of Assessment*. Oxon: Routledge. p. 145.

[59] **D. Reay & D. Wiliam** (1999). 'I'll be a nothing': Structure, agency and the construction of identity through assessment. *British Educational Research Journal*, 25(3), 43–354.

The education system we are stuck with is the one we have to deal with – however, teachers can adapt their practice to make assessment as meaningful and formative as possible.

Where summative assessment fits in

Using the assessment model, we can see where summative tests or exams fit into the system and how they can be used to inform teaching and learning. Look at figure 2i1, and notice the opportunities in lessons to use test items. Summative assessment has an important role in classroom assessment, but it is often overemphasised and used instead of formative assessment. The figure shows that tests can have a formative role within the classroom assessment framework, if the feedback loop is returned to inform the teacher on their teaching and the learners on their learning.

 Also see

This section builds on 2c) Planning meaningful assessment.

It also has links with these sections when using test items formatively:

- 2f) Developing meaningful success criteria and rubrics

- 2g) Giving meaningful and effective feedback

- 2h) Meaningful self- and peer assessment.

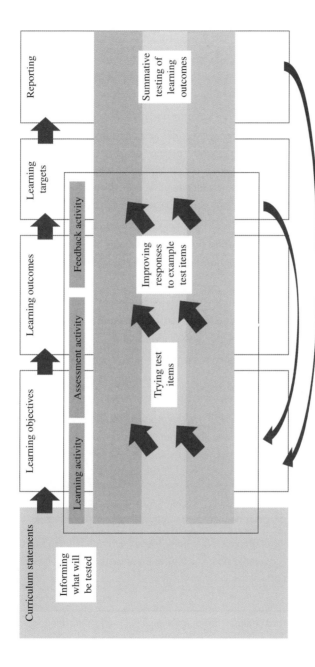

Figure 21: A model for classroom assessment: Where using summative tests fits in

Giving marks and comments

 **Evidence**

This research is considered seminal, as it was the first study to demonstrate the detrimental effects of giving learners marks for their work, rather than just comments. The experimental design and statistical significance gave significant insight into extrinsic and intrinsic motivation of learners when it comes to teacher feedback.

Black and Wiliam used this research paper as a case study in their formative assessment review paper (section 1c) and, since then, there has been ongoing debate about whether or not we should give learners marks.[60, 61] It is a classic demonstration that, despite what educational research shows, cultural practices of schooling, education and assessment are so deeply embedded they are very hard to shift.

Therefore, I think every teacher should be aware of this paper, reflect on their own practice and think about the implications of giving grades to learners in everyday lessons.

Butler, R. (1987). Task-involving and ego-involving properties of evaluation: effects of different feedback conditions on motivational perceptions, interest and performance. *Journal of Educational Psychology*, 79, 474–482.

The research predicted, based on theories of motivation, that after doing a task:

- Teacher comments would encourage learners to be focused on the task: 'task involvement'.

- Both grades and praise would promote 'ego involvement'.

Research questions

The general thesis that comments would promote task involvement, that both grades and praise would promote ego involvement, and that no feedback would promote neither, yielded several specific hypotheses:

1 Attributions of effort, outcomes, and the effects of evaluation to task-involved factors would be highest after comments; attributions to ego-involved factors would be highest, and similar, after grades and after

---

[60] **E. Smith & S. Gorard** (2005). 'They don't give us our marks': the role of formative feedback in student progress. *Assessment in Education: Principles, Policy & Practice*, 12(1), 21–38.

[61] **P. Black, C. Harrison, J. Hodgen, B. Marshall & D. Wiliam** (2005). The dissemination of formative assessment: a lesson from, or about, evaluation. *Research Intelligence*, 92, 14–15.

praise; and attributions to both kinds of causes would be lowest after no feedback.

2 Interest and performance at post-test (session 3) would be higher after comments than after grades, praise, or no feedback. Interest and performance in the latter three conditions would be similar.

3 These effects for attributions, interest, and performance would occur at both high and low levels of school achievement.

Method

School students were classified as high achievers or low achievers and were given tasks that encouraged divergent thinking:

- Session 1 – students did a pre-test and were not told they would get feedback.

- Session 2 – the session 1 task was returned with task-related comments, numerical grades, or praise. The students did a new task and were told they would get the same types of feedback.

- Session 3 – session 2 tasks were given back with the same categories of feedback/no feedback. Session 3 task was administered with no feedback expected.

Findings

The headlines were as follows:

1 Effort, outcomes, and the effects of evaluation to task-involved factors were the highest after comments alone. Grades alone or grades and comments scored lower for all attributes.

2 Interest and performance at post-test (session 3) were higher after comments than after grades, praise, or no feedback.

3 The effects for attributions, interest, and performance did occur at both high and low levels of school achievement in most cases.

Phases towards using summative tests formatively

Figure 2i2 represents the suggested phases making lesson objectives effective for fostering a formative assessment culture. Each phase is linked to the practices I will discuss in the rest of this section.

To help you establish which phase you are in, and how to develop your practice, use the following questionnaire (table 2i1).

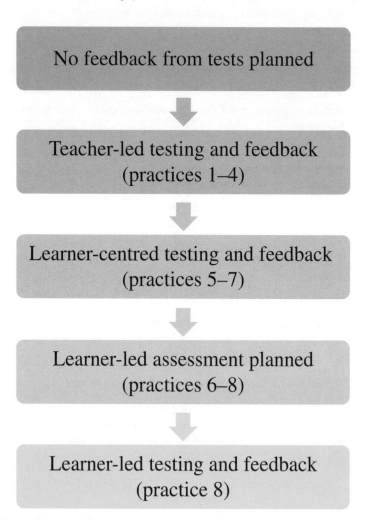

Figure 2i2: Towards using summative tests, formatively

Practice analyser: Towards using summative tests formatively

Go through the questionnaire and, for each statement, tick the box that best illustrates your use of that practice.

Table 2i1: Practice analyser: Towards using summative tests formatively

	Practice	Regularly	Often	Sometimes	Rarely	Never
1	Tests done – results given					
2	Test results used to inform next steps for teaching					
3	Time given to going through answers of a test					
4	Test results used to inform next steps for learning					
5	Exemplar test questions given to try before the actual test					
6	Exemplar test questions given to try and improve upon before the actual test					
7	Learners given the mark scheme after the test to attempt to self-mark					
8	Learners create their own test questions and answers					

To analyse your results, first identify the best-fit description for your practices. For example, are your responses mostly in the 'rarely' or 'never' categories? If so, you are likely to be in the 'teacher-led marking and feedback' phase, so you would benefit from reading and applying practices 1–4. But first, here is some more information on practices and potential next steps.

Analysing your practice and deciding your next steps

Having established the practices you use, decide which practice you would like to develop. Note that the practices at the top of the list are more likely to happen within a classroom with a summative culture, and they get progressively more likely to happen in a formative one.

Think about your school assessment culture and your assessment beliefs and values, so that you can make an achievable next step to improve your classroom assessment practice.

Mostly 'rarely'/'never'

If you do not give feedback from tests beyond the grade achieved, then the next step is to try to identify some teacher-led feedback opportunities after a test (practices 1–4). This will help your learners have more involvement with the assessment process and be able to analyse what they got wrong and how to improve. Depending on the culture of your school and classroom, you may wish to start with practices 5–7. This will enable you and your learners to develop a more formative culture, with feedback from summative tests being more learner-centred.

Mostly 'sometimes'

If you sometimes do most of these practices, choose one or two you would like to develop next. Carefully think about your school and classroom culture and consider which practices might benefit you in developing a more formative culture and improve teaching, learning and assessment in your lessons. You may want to focus on improving just one practice, such as using strategies to use test results to inform the next steps in learning (practice 4), or using exemplar test questions formatively before a test is done (practice 6).

Mostly 'regularly'/'often'

In the case of mostly 'regularly'/'often' answers; if you have identified a practice that is 'sometimes', perhaps this is the one you may wish to develop, especially if it is lower down the table. Next, if you are already using each of these practices, you may want to evaluate how effectively you are using them. Reading one of the sections may help you analyse your implementation and give you new ideas to try and develop.

If you have fully established these practices, then look at another section of Chapter 2 to see what you might like to improve.

 Reflection

Consider the scope for using summative tests formatively. Decide on *one* area of practice that would help improve your classroom assessment. Consider the constraints you have from your school culture and your aspirations for a more formative classroom. Think what is achievable and what is likely to have the most success and impact on teaching, learning and assessment.

- Read the pages that relate to that practice or set of practices.
- Choose one class to trial the activities with.
- Reflect on how your practice has changed and the impact on teaching, learning and assessment.

Test done – results given (practice 1)

Traditionally, teachers give tests, mark tests and give back the results – often as a series of ticks and crosses, numbers, and a score or grade. The learner looks at the grade, will have some form of emotional response, either positive or negative; is likely to have a motivational response, either positive or negative; and, more often than not, moves on to the next topic without a second thought. A step towards being formative would be for the teacher to analyse the test, work out what most learners had difficulty answering, and plan a lesson to address those mistakes (practice 2). Even better if the teacher spends some time engaging learners with the test answers; this will at least focus them on what they got right and wrong (practice 3). More efficient and effective would be identifying the next steps in learning and allowing learners time to correct what they got wrong (practice 4).

Test results used to inform next steps for teaching (practice 2)

As a teacher, when I mark a set of tests I notice what learners commonly got wrong. I then have a choice of addressing those mistakes with the class, or just noting that I need to teach this better next time I do that topic. I think many teachers do a bit of both. Sometimes, with assessments such as mock exams or end-of-topic tests, teachers can be more systematic about the analysis of the test, either by using a tally to see which learners scored what for each individual question, or by constructing a spreadsheet. This can then inform the teacher of the learners' areas of strength and the areas that need more time and focus to improve. Although this practice has formative qualities (in that it is identifying gaps in knowledge and understanding) the process is in the teacher's control. The test is being done to the learners; the learners are the recipients of the teacher's analysis. This will work in more traditional classrooms, but there is opportunity to involve the learner with the practice (practices 3 and 4).

Time given to going through test answers (practice 3)

Involving learners in looking through their marked test is a way in which to help them understand what they got wrong. This can be done well by experienced teachers who use a series of questions to develop learners' ideas on the spot to arrive at the correct answers. However, the learners who got that question right in the test are sitting doing nothing. These can be rather drawn-out processes too, and can be made more efficient (see practice 4).

Test results used to inform next steps for learning (practice 4)

When a test or mock exam takes place, an effective follow-up is to focus on what each learner got wrong and give them support with corrections and improvements. This should be done in a non-judgemental way, ensuring that the expectations are shared ahead of the test, and explaining that there will be feedback and time for making corrections and improvements. It could be done as follows. The learners sit the test; the teacher marks it, then gives back the marked test papers the next lesson. The teacher summarises what everyone did well and lets the class know that there were some common mistakes. The teacher prepares a grid like that in table 2i2, to provide improvement activities for specific questions that learners got wrong. Learners should only be expected to try two or three improvements, because otherwise it could be overwhelming. Teachers should also consider providing an extension activity for those who only made one or two errors.

Table 2i2: An example of guidance for learners to make improvements

Structured, learning-focused improvement time		
Test questions	Knowledge, understanding or skill area	Support (improvement activities)
1, 4 and 6	Knowledge and understanding 1 and 2	Textbook A, pages 24–26
2 and 7	Knowledge area 4	Worksheet C
3, 5 and 8	Knowledge and understanding 3 and 5	Textbook A, pages 27–29
9 and 10	Skill 1	Practise skill using information sheet Z
Extension activity	Extending skill 1	Read passage in textbook C and try questions

Exemplar test questions given to try before the actual test (practice 5)

Most examinations have a certain style of question. Whether these are multiple-choice or essay questions, there is a set of rules the learners need to understand to be able to answer a question correctly. With most examinations, subject knowledge, understanding and skills are not enough. Exam technique is a skill to be taught and learned.

One of my concerns about school education is that in some countries the schooling process just becomes one long lead-up to final exams. Education become dominated by passing exams at the expense of more meaningful development of a love of learning, a critical interest in the subjects and the human condition, a thirst for self-improvement, and curiosity for life. However, learners do, at some point, need to learn how to answer exam questions themselves.

Developing exam technique requires learners to understand the rules, and teachers often become good at tutoring learners on how to maximise marks. For example, in science, learners are encouraged to always put the relevant units after a quantity, and in mathematics, to show workings and use the appropriate number of decimal places.

To make the process more formative and learner-centred, learners could either compile or make a checklist (see section 2f) that they refer to regularly to self-assess or peer assess answers to questions.

Exemplar test questions tried and improved on before the actual test (practice 6)

This simple method uses relevant exemplar exam questions at the end of a lesson or learning episode. This is illustrated in the classroom case study later in this section. In this situation, the purpose of the activity needs to be clear. Learners need to understand that they are practising exam questions in order to assess what they can do and to take opportunities to make improvements.

This is a form of revision and can focus on both exam technique and exam content. To encourage the process to be more learner-led, encourage peer assessment activities that allow learners to see each other's answers (see section 2h). In doing this, learners can learn from each other in producing a good answer to an exam question.

Using exemplar test questions 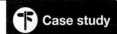 **Case study**

Elena is a secondary school history teacher in England. She shared with me a lesson in which she carried out 'key question' assessments. With her year 10 class (aged 14–15), the learners complete 'end of key question assessments' after finishing the content in each section – or key question – of the module. These assessments were modelled on the final national assessments (GCSE). In the 'crime and punishment through time' module, students answered a four-mark question, a 12-mark question and a 20-mark question. The course is taught chronologically and focuses on four time periods. Following the assessment for one of these (Industrial Britain), Elena delivered a feedback lesson in which examples of students' good practice were shared with the class, and her guidance on how the questions should have been answered was given. This included ideas on the possible content they might have included, and the structure they might have used for their answers. This took around 30 minutes of the lesson – Elena made sure that students were given the opportunity to dissect other students' answers, so that they could see exactly how and why they had been successful.

Following this first part of the lesson, Elena gave students around 20–30 minutes to rewrite or improve at least one of their answers. Several of the students addressed the four-mark question, as they had misunderstood it (they thought it was asking them about means of transport, rather than transportation as a form of punishment). Other students attempted to write one or two paragraphs of the 20-mark question, responding to feedback about structure. Elena made it clear that she wanted to take in these rewritten pieces of work and look at them, which seemed to give students clearer focus in the lesson.

Two students took it upon themselves to improve their assessments outside of the lesson. One managed to improve her answer by 40 per cent, achieving 94 per cent in her fully rewritten assessment, and the other demonstrated a much clearer understanding of how to structure his paragraphs in the 20-mark question.

Learners given the mark scheme after the test to attempt to self-mark (practice 7)

Most examinations come with a mark scheme. Using the mark scheme with learners in preparation for examinations gives them ownership and understanding. Transparency leads to a clear understanding of what is expected of them. Marking their own answers against the mark scheme helps learners to see why an answer was wrong and the process by which they will be assessed. It will also give an opportunity to discuss any misunderstandings (there are often situations where learners misread the question, or miss a key word), learn how to structure answers, and gain a sense of what the examiner is looking for. An extension to this type of activity is to encourage learners to make their own test questions and mark scheme from test questions, described in practice 8.

Learners create their own test questions and answers (practice 8)

As a revision exercise, learners can be encouraged to write questions that they think might be asked, along with the mark scheme, then swap them

Using a textbook and an exemplar question, they can produce the types of question they could be asked and the answers that may be expected.

As with writing success criteria and rubrics (section 2f), test questions take a lot of skill to write. However, if learners focus on the type of question, the active verb, the key words, and concepts required for the answer, it will help them better understand the rules of the examination game. When learners are becoming more independent, confident and self-regulating, this type of exercise gives them ownership over the tools by which they will be examined.

 How to

To use summative tests formatively, teachers should:

- plan how to feed back individually to learners once the tests have been marked

- provide structured time and supporting resources for learners to improve and make corrections

- use assessment data to inform their teaching of their current class and future classes

- utilise exemplar exam questions and mark schemes to give learners an opportunity to understand how to answer exam questions

- encourage peer assessment of practice questions to learn from each other how to answer a test item

- as revision activities, challenge learners to write test items and mark schemes to test each other.

Chapter 3

The future of assessment

3a) Reflections on the classroom assessment model

This book reflects current education practice in the UK and some other parts of the world. It is even more a reflection of my thoughts and understanding of classroom assessment. I wonder, if I have the opportunity to write a second edition in five or ten years, how much my thinking will have changed. So I encourage you to read this book critically and question it.

I have presented pretty much what I present to my trainee teachers, schools and educational organisations when I am coaching, mentoring or advising. I have focused on what a teacher can do to make their assessment practices more formative and learner-centred – I have not considered changes in the school, nor the educational system. That is beyond the scope of this guide.

Teachers hold a lot of power within their classroom. They can influence its culture by sharing their expectations and using practices that provide opportunities for formative practices. Teachers can decide if they will make assessment teacher-led, learner-centred or learner-led. Their attitudes, beliefs and practices will influence the attitudes, beliefs and practices of their learners. While accepting the objective, statistical, systematic nature of external high-stakes assessment, teachers can accept classroom assessment as a social process that is more subjective, fuzzy and personal in nature.

At the end of this book, however, it is important to recognise the importance of change happening beyond the classroom.

3b) Educational change

This book focuses on the changes that teachers can make in their own classrooms, often despite the assessment culture they work in. Although this can be effective on the small scale, large-scale educational change requires systemic change. There needs to be political will, but also there needs to be support from teaching professionals themselves.

The trouble with politicians being involved with decisions in education is that they mostly have little more experience of schools and education than their own school experience. A single politician can cause chaos in a country's educational system just by making ill-judged or ideologically-motivated policy change. It seems to me that the single best thing for the education system would be to decouple it from the state. Although the education authority should be accountable to the state, it should not be controlled by it.

Political structures have a huge influence and have their own challenges. I have a democratic experience, but have worked in countries with authoritarian regimes. Having been involved in educational reform in Kazakhstan, I could really appreciate the level of planning enabled by a political system that was less likely to change. The Kazakhs have a 20-year plan for educational reform, reaching out across the world for the best practices, building some flagship schools, then rolling them out over the years. The system is not perfect, and there are many challenges. However, I envy the ability to plan long term in developing the educational system, rather than over the four-to-five-year political cycle here in the UK. Change could perhaps be achieved with a decoupling of the educational authority from party politics in democratic countries.

Helping teachers change their practice must involve engaging them in the process of change. In Beijing, I took part in some teacher training: a five-day course delivered to teachers who were allocated to the course by the education authority. There was no agency for these teachers; they did not have any particular desire to improve their practice in assessment for learning, and although they were quite receptive, I suspect most went back to their classrooms after the summer break having forgotten much of what they were taught.

In contrast, an action research programme was rolled out as part of the Kazakhstan reform that invited teachers to engage in developing a part of their practice. Working in small groups, with a research lead, they could explore, challenge and change their own practice. Many of the teachers involved with this programme were passionate about their research and there was clear impact on their professional identity, teaching and learning.

I am an advocate of collaborative action research over a sustained period, with expert input. This motivates teachers, gives them deep understanding of the changes they are making, and has far more chance of embedding new practices. The caution is that the practices being embedded need to be research informed and evidence based, to ensure that they have potential effectiveness.

3c) **Alternative assessment**

Early in my career I was unquestioning about educational policy and practice. As I became more experienced, more inquisitive and less satisfied with the system, I became more critical. I have been fortunate to be able to think beyond the status quo, and I realise that the way assessment is done in schools is not the only way – in fact, the way schooling is done is not the only way.

Formative assessment has been debated for years and continues to be questioned and refined,[62] particularly as different political agendas take hold. However, I can see pockets of alternative thought and alternative systems around the world, and hope that one day they will become the norm.

In this section, I want to share with you some resources that have helped me challenge my thinking about education and the role of assessment within that. Here, I introduce five books that will challenge your thinking. Even if you choose just one to read, I promise it will make you start to question what we do.

My involvement with the Perimeter Institute's Learning 2030 summit revealed to me that we can tackle education differently and build learning environments that are not schools, and that have different assumptions and structures. I have promoted my learner-centred assessment agenda in this book, and I hope this is the future. What I haven't dwelt on is the harmful impact of our current assessment systems on the mental health of learners and teachers. *De-testing and De-grading Schools*, an edited book by Canadian educators Joe Bower and Paul Thomas, exposes these issues. The authors make the case that teachers, learners and parents are addicted to grades and need to be weaned off them through 'cold turkey'. They describe how this can be done through real examples of authentic alternatives.[63]

From the perspective of alternative assessment systems, these ideas are already being discussed. In the UK, Guy Claxon, a professor in education,

---

[62] **D. Christodoulou** (2017). *Making Good Progress? The Future of Assessment for Learning*. Oxford: Oxford University Press.

[63] **J. Bower & P.L. Thomas (Eds.)** (2016). *De-testing and De-grading Schools: Authentic alternatives to accountability and standardization*. New York: Peter Lang.

argues for a focus on the development and assessment of 'habits of mind', which focus on learning how to learn and on the skills required to function in life and society. In the United States, Linda Darling-Hammond, a professor at Stanford University, offers an alternative assessment model based on performance assessments. Her book, *Next Generation Assessment: Moving Beyond the Bubble Test*, is highly accessible to teachers and sets out thought-provoking issues and alternatives.[64]

As I have explained, teaching, learning and assessment are intricately linked. Together, they form the curriculum. Two short books explore alternative styles of school systems: the first explores 'the democratic route' of education and the second an 'aims-based curriculum' with a focus on 'human flourishing'. Frank Coffield and Bill Williamson, in their book *From Exam Factories to Communities of Discovery*, make a call for a more democratic system that is able to challenge local and global threats of environmental change, social inequalities, and global competition. They offer a just and sustainable model of education.[65] Michael Reiss and John White also challenge the status quo and question what schools should be for. They offer a curriculum that is based not on subjects, but on the elements of human flourishing. They go on to discuss how this could be possible in the current political and global educational climate.[66]

Finally, I want to mention the work of Graham Brown-Martin. I met Graham at the Learning 2030 summit in Canada. He is very passionate about education and, among other things, has produced a book called *Learning {Re}Imagined*.[67] For me, this is more of an event than a book. It has links to videos of interviews with the leading thinkers and doers in education from around the world. It is a truly global exploration of what education is and what it could be. Graham is a controversial, provocative voice in the educational arena who has challenged me to really think about my assumptions of what schools do now and what they could be.

---

[64] **L. Darling-Hammond** (2014). *Next Generation Assessment: Moving beyond the bubble test to support 21st century learning*. San Francisco: Jossey-Bass.

[65] **F. Coffield & B. Williamson** (2011). *From Exam Factories to Communities of Discovery*. London: Institute of Education, University of London.

[66] **M. Reiss & J. White** (2013). *An Aims-based Curriculum: The significance of human flourishing for schools*. London: IOE Press.

[67] **G. Brown-Martin.** (2014). *Learning {Re}Imagined: How the connected society is transforming learning*. Qatar: Bloomsbury.

3d) Making progress

Although these opportunities are exciting, interesting, and sometimes even frightening, it is unlikely that they will happen overnight. So it is pertinent to think how we can make the best of the assessment system we are stuck with. I hope that this book offers a pragmatic approach to moving forward with formative practices, and developing learners who are more self-confident and self-regulating, whatever the culture of your country and school.

There is a movement in the UK that is focused on the idea of progress: how learners progress through subjects; how we measure progress; and what progress looks like. This has become something of an obsession in schools, and there are a number of models that vary in academic and educational value. The idea of progress links closely to assessment. It requires teachers to have robust models of progression, structures that can assess and feedback, and effective interventions. This I will discuss in my next book in this series.

Index

Index of figures

Index of tables

Acknowledgements

Badger Publishing Ltd for extract from *Badger Key Stage 3 Science: Level-Assessed Tasks – for Year 7*, Grevatt, A. (2005). 7G task sheet (L3–5). Reproduced with permission from Badger Publishing Ltd

Badger Publishing Ltd for extract from *Physics Homework Tasks with Learning Ladder*, Chandler-Grevatt A. and Stutt, V. (2009). 'Making and Presenting 2' ACE Learning Ladder – Solar Shoeboxes. Reproduced with permission from Badger Publishing Ltd.

Pearson Education, Inc. for two tables from *A Taxonomy for Learning, Teaching, and Assessing: A Revision of Bloom's Taxonomy of Educational Objectives*, Anderson, L. W. et al. (2001). Pages 28 and 31. Reproduced with permission from Pearson Education, Inc., (New York, New York).

SAGE Publications Ltd for two figures from *Assessment of Learning*, Harlen, W. (2007). Pages 120 and 122. Reproduced with permission of SAGE Publications Ltd.

Springer for figure 4 from *Formative Assessment and Science Education*, Bell, B. and Cowie, B. (2001). Page 91. Reproduced with permission from Springer.

Notes